SHAMBHALA DRAGON EDITIONS

The dragon is an age-old symbol of the highest spiritual essence, embodying wisdom, strength, and the divine power of transformation. In this spirit, Shambhala Dragon Editions offers a treasury of readings in the sacred knowledge of Asia. In presenting the works of authors both ancient and modern, we seek to make these teachings accessible to lovers of wisdom everywhere.

KENSHO

The Heart of Zen

Thomas Cleary

SHAMBHALA

Boston & London

1997

SHAMBHALA PUBLICATIONS, INC.
Horticultural Hall
300 Massachusetts Avenue
Boston, Massachusetts 02115

9 8 7 6 5 4 3 2 1

FIRST EDITION
Printed in the United States of America
♾ This edition is printed on acid-free paper that meets the
American National Standards Institute z39.48 Standard.
Distributed in the United States by Random House, Inc.,
and in Canada by Random House of Canada Ltd

Library of Congress Cataloging-in-Publication Data
Kensho: the heart of Zen/Thomas Cleary.—1st ed.
    p. cm.
ISBN 1-57062-269-8 (alk. paper)
1. Spiritual life—Zen Buddhism. 2. Enlightenment (Zen Buddhism)
I. Cleary, Thomas F., 1949– .
BQ9288.K46   1996   96-18728
294.3'927—dc20   CIP

Contents

PART THREE: *Zen Koans*

Introduction

Zen Buddhism emerged in China fifteen hundred years ago as a gnostic revival of Buddhism. According to tradition, Zen was, in essence, originally a response to the spiritual sterility into which Buddhism had fallen through formalism.

The special focus of the Zen dispensation was publicized by the famous Hui-neng, who is associated with the founding of the so-called Sudden school of Zen in China nearly thirteen hundred years ago:

> The complete discourses of all Buddhas of past, present, and future are inherent in the essence of the human being. If you cannot realize this on your own, you need the guidance of a teacher to see it. As for those who do realize on their own, they do not need to seek elsewhere.
>
> If you insist that a teacher is necessary to attain liberation, you are wrong. Why? Because there is a teacher within your own mind who enlightens you spontaneously!
>
> If you create confusion, false thinking, and delusion, even a teacher's instruction cannot save you!
>
> If you cultivate the observant perception of true insight, then false thoughts die out at once. And if you know your own essence, with this one realization you arrive at enlightenment.

In Sino-Japanese, this Zen insight into the essence of one's own being is called *kensho*. There is no Zen without kensho; complete kensho is what is known as satori, Zen awakening. This realization is likened to finding an inexhaustible treasure, for it means the awakening of the whole potential for the experience of experience itself.

The Zen master Dogen, who brought Zen to Japan nearly eight centuries ago, explained the heart of Zen to a layman in his famous essay "The Issue at Hand":

> Learning the way of enlightenment is learning selfhood.
> Learning selfhood is forgetting oneself.
> Forgetting oneself is being enlightened by all things.

In Zen, the meaning of the true self is none other than Buddha-nature, which Buddhist scripture defines as "Pure, Blissful, Permanent Selfhood."

To learn about the self in Zen means to study the false self, or the ego, and the true self, or Buddha-nature. Learning selfhood, in Zen terms, means learning to see through the doings of the ego's self-image in order to find the nature of the real self as it is in itself, by itself.

Seeing through the doings of the vain and suggestive ego makes it possible to be immune to its seductions. This is a kind of "forgetting oneself," in the sense of leaving behind the foibles of this vanity.

Finding the nature of the real self makes it possible to *be* oneself, without self-consciously trying. This is also "forgetting oneself," in the sense of leaving behind self-importance.

When egocentric rationalizations do not occupy the mind, then actualities can inform it. When spontaneous awareness opens the mind, then realities can instruct it. The awakened Zen self is like a mirror as big as cosmic space, reflecting the whole universe within it.

The popular fourteenth-century Japanese preacher Keizan described this Zen practice and experience over and over in his classic *Transmission of Light*: "Even if you seem to be a beginner, if the mind is turned around for a moment to reveal its originally inherent qualities, nothing at all is lacking. Together with the realized ones, you will commune with all Buddhas."

The Zen canon is the most voluminous of all Buddhist canons, but there is no standard course or text of Zen. Neither is there any standard dogma, ritual, or practice given in authentic Zen teaching, for as one of the great teachers used to say, "Awakening is the rule." Certain particular works, nonetheless, focus on the essential experience of kensho in such explicit detail that they provide useful introductions to the subject for lay people.

Among the traditional Zen works devoted to kensho are a number of important texts attributed to some of the greatest Zen preachers of China, Korea, and Japan. The *Altar Scripture*, believed to be discourses of Hui-neng, founder of the Sudden school, is one such. *Transmission of Light*, cited earlier, and *Dream Dialogues*, slightly older, are two famous examples of Japanese kensho manuals.

All of these texts are book-length works, each in a different format. No school is actually based on any one of them, but all of them are commonly read by people interested in Zen. There are also a number of shorter works on kensho by famous Zen preachers, which focus even more intensely on kensho and the intricacies and subtleties of its realization and integration.

Straightforward Explanation of the True Mind, by the Korean Zen preacher Chinul (1158–1210), is one of the most accessible of all Zen texts. Relating Zen kensho to teachings of Buddhist scriptures and treatises, Chinul lends contextual balance to the understanding and experience of awakening. Chinul had no specific teacher, and attained awakening working with Buddhist scripture; both spiritually and historically he was clearly affected by the residual influence of the work of the Fa-yen school of Zen, which had been active in China and Korea in the ninth and tenth centuries. Korean Zen was particularly indebted to the work of the third grand master of the Fa-yen school, Yung-ming Yen-shou, especially through his magnum opus *Source Mirror Record*, his valued opuscule *Secrets of Mind Alone*, and his many Korean disciples.

The Zen school of which Chinul is considered the founder eventually stagnated spiritually through oversimplification, irrationality, extremism, and worldly influences. Many of these problems stemmed from neglect of the greater balance of Chinul's own teaching, an irony not untypical in the history of religions. The works that Chinul himself authored, nevertheless, remain as classic introductions to Zen fundamentals, even if they are no longer necessarily learned or practiced by all followers of Chinul's school.

Straightforward Explanation of the True Mind is one of Chinul's most valuable works. It consists of fifteen chapters, approaching the subject of kensho from the point of view of its object, cultivation, function, and consequences. Composed in a very simple Chinese style, this work contains many references to scriptures, treatises, and classical Zen lore, helping the reader to connect the experience of kensho with Buddhism in general in order to highlight the critical technical information available in a wide variety of Buddhist literature.

The most prolific writer on kensho in later times is undoubtedly the famous Japanese Zen preacher Hakuin (1686–1769). Hakuin is one of the best-known names in Zen as it is known in the West, in spite of the fact that relatively little of his work has been introduced here, and its use in modern Japanese Zen sects claiming spiritual descent from Hakuin is also quite limited. As in the case of Chinul, nonetheless, Hakuin's works remain useful sources of technical assistance in the cultivation and application of Zen insight.

Born into a time when Zen in Japan had been decadent for centuries, Hakuin suffered greatly in his youthful quest for enlightenment, even to the point where he experienced complete mental and physical breakdown. He was able to study with the person he considered his real teacher for only eight months, while he was in his twenties, and also claimed not to have fully understood his teacher until he himself was in his forties.

As his works show, even after many great and small awakenings Hakuin continued to pursue complete enlightenment relentlessly, using the intricacies of Buddhist scripture and Zen lore to open the hidden resources of spiritual perception. His work never loses the stridency and urgency of tone, with a sharp critical edge, that betoken the aspect of pain and bewilderment in Hakuin's life, first in his personal quest and then later in facing a world of form drained of content.

Hakuin emphasized kensho very strongly in his works, yet he is equally adamant about the importance of going even further to cultivate constructive integration with the ordinary world by applying Zen insight to the full range of human experience. Hakuin himself was also an amateur painter and calligrapher, as well as a poet and a writer. His own versatility won him many friends of all kinds, from samurai lords to local merchants and farmers, including countless followers of his progressive Zen study as well as scholars of other traditions.

A central problem faced by both Chinul and Hakuin, along with innumerable other students of Zen, was the deterioration of tradition and loss of authentic transmission. This was most keenly felt in the rarity of genuine teachers and the obscurity of the koans used to orient advanced studies.

The seeming paradox of the teacherhood issue is that, according to unimpeachable classical sources like Pai-chang, Lin-chi, Yun-men, and Fo-yen, someone who claims to be a Zen teacher is not. This does not present quite the problem it may appear to, for the consequence of this principle is that the parties to any sort of willing interaction do in fact need to exercise their own perceptions and accept their own responsibilities for what they are doing.

The irony in the obscurity of koans is that it derives mainly from linguistic and contextual gaps between sectarian Zen in Korea and Japan on the one hand and comprehensive classical Chinese Zen on the other. Offshoots of Korean and Japanese sects, not understanding the structure of the koans, have tended to make this aspect of Zen into a cult of secrecy, mystery, and/or simple mystification.

Imported to the West, this type of cult has given rise to the new coinage *koanophobia*, "fear of koans," evidently on account of their exploitation for bafflement value. Added to the premise of koanic secrets of overwhelming importance held authoritatively by an autocratic potentate and an elite circle, in a cultural environment where self-esteem is considered a central value, the mystery-cult approach to koans has had the effect of intimidating and yet alluring those who are naive or inwardly uncommitted but nevertheless wish to think well of themselves.

As with certain other materials from the Zen canon, the neglect or misuse of thousands of koans has not caused them to pass out of existence. The keys to their meanings, which are both scattered and concentrated throughout the scriptures and treatises of classical Buddhism as well as Chinese Zen lore itself, also remain in existence regardless of their use, disuse, or abuse. Buddhists call this phenomenon a *dharmakaya*, or "Body of Teaching," that remains through time regardless of the existence or demise of any *sambhogakaya*, or "Body of Enjoyment" of the teaching, or any *nirmanakaya*, or "Body of Projection" of the teaching.

One of many great koan collections whose living enjoyment and projection passed away while its body of teachings remains is the noble *Book of Ease*. This is a collection of prose and verse commentaries on one hundred Zen koans. The verse comments were composed by a twelfth-century Zen master known by the place name of T'ien-t'ung. The prose comments were written for a layman by a thirteenth-century Zen master known by the place name of Wan-sung.

In contrast to the obscure and often obtuse comments on koans made by latter-day cultists of the irrationalist persuasion, classical Zen masters of China made lucid structural analyses and analogical explanations of the koans as early as the ninth century. A koan, meaning an "objective example," is like a technical formula, a design, representing Buddhist teaching in a highly concentrated form. Recollection of koans facilitates the ongoing practice of Buddhist meditations in the midst of ordinary wordly activities, once a popular Zen technique.

The present volume is designed to introduce the bases of Zen according to traditional materials and methods designed for the lay individual.

The thirteenth-century Zen master Dogen, one of the founders of Zen in Japan, wrote of Zen in ordinary life in these terms: "In present-day China, the rulers, ministers, and intellectuals, both men and women, all set their hearts on Zen. Warriors and scholars both aspire to Zen. Certainly many of those who aspire do illumine the ground of mind, so it is evident that worldly duties do not hinder the way to enlightenment."

PART ONE

THE TRUE MIND

Chinul's

Straightforward Explanation

of the True Mind

Faith

In Buddhism, faith is understood as a faculty (Sanskrit, *indriya*) that can be developed into a power *(bala)*. This faculty, this power, enables seekers to reach toward what they have not yet experienced or personally realized.

Insofar as Buddhist faith, as a faculty and a power, is not an absolute commitment to dogma or ritual, different dispositions of faith can be employed within Buddhism. In Chinul's explanations of the true mind, the power of the faculty of faith is focused on the intrinsic identity of the essence of mind itself with the essence of Buddhahood.

Chinul insists on the need for faith as the first step of the journey to awakening. He adds that the first step must be correct if the journey is to lead to the goal. Thus faith has to be combined with understanding. Yet even with intellectual understanding, the power of faith is still indispensible, because the mind still does not know itself—it is still charmed by its own thoughts.

Only when understanding becomes realization does the faculty of faith have the power to conduct consciousness all the way to experiential truth. Yet the power of faith inwardly supports the capacity to experience and realize truth, so the quality and direction of faith must first be examined. Here is Chinul's explanation of the place of faith in Zen.

Right Faith in the True Mind

The *Flower Ornament Scripture* says, "Faith is the source of the path, the mother of virtues, nurturing all roots of goodness." Also, the *Treatise on Only Representation* says, "Faith is like a water-clarifying crystal, able to clear murky waters." So we know that faith guides the development of all goodness. This is why Buddhist scriptures begin with the words, "Thus have I heard."

Some people ask about a difference between faith as it is in the context of Zen and faith as it is in the context of pan-Buddhism. There are many different kinds of faith. Buddhism tells people who believe in causality and who like happiness to have faith in ten virtues as sublime causes, and to have faith in humanity and higher states as pleasant results. For those who enjoy empty quietude, belief in the conditions of birth and death is the right cause, while the way to extinction of causes of misery is the holy result. For those who like complete Buddhahood, faith in the six perfections over three aeons is the great cause; enlightenment and nirvana are the great results.

In Zen, however, right faith is not the same as any of these. One does not have faith in any contrived causes or effects; it is only necessary to have faith that the intrinsic self is originally Buddha. The natural true intrinsic essence is complete in all people; the subtle substance of nirvana is perfect in every individual. It is not to be sought from another; it has been there all along.

The third patriarch of Zen said, "It is complete as space, with no lack or excess; it is just because of grasping and rejecting that you are not thus." Master Chih said, "It is the formless body in the body of form, the road of the uncreated on the road of ignorance." Yung-chia said, "The true essence of ignorance is none other than the essence of enlightenment; the ephemeral body is none other than the spiritual body." So we know that people are originally Buddhas.

Once you have developed right faith, it is necessary to understand it. Yung-ming said, "Faith without understanding increases ignorance; understanding without faith increases subjective opinions." So we know that we can gain access to the path rapidly when faith and understanding are combined.

Some ask whether there is any benefit when one has just awakened faith but cannot yet enter the path. The *Treatise on Awakening of Faith* says, "If people do not become cowardly on hearing this teaching, they will certainly succeed to the Buddhas, and will certainly be given direction by the Buddhas. Even if someone can induce all be-

4

ings in the universe to behave well, that is not as good as someone correctly contemplating this teaching for one moment of thought." Also, a *Scripture on Transcendent Wisdom* says, "Any who conceive pure faith for even a moment are known to Buddha and seen by Buddha, one and all." So people gain infinite blessings like this. Obviously, if you are going to make a journey of a thousand miles, the first step has to be right; if the first step is mistaken, the whole thousand miles is mistaken. To enter the land where there is no artificiality, first faith has to be right; if the initial belief is mistaken, then all virtues fade away. This is why a Zen patriarch said, "The slightest miss is as the distance between sky and earth."

Terminology

Even though the setup of Zen faith may differ in structure from those of other Buddhist schools based on scriptures and classical treatises, nevertheless the true mind, or Buddha-mind, which is the object of Zen faith, is also represented in those very scriptures and treatises that form the bases of the doctrinal schools.

Chinul makes this abundantly clear with a list of numerous terms from numerous texts, all pointing to the true mind. He goes on to add another long list of special Zen names. Each name, furthermore, is accompanied by a reason for the name, which is generally a representation of a function, the function a pattern of practice. As in his essay on faith, in his essay on terminology Chinul combines understanding with absorption to elicit the Zen effect.

Different Names for the True Mind

It may be asked, now that we have conceived right faith, what is the true mind? To this it may be replied that detachment from falsehood is called truth, while awareness is called mind. This mind is elucidated in the *Lankavatara Scripture*. It may be asked, is it only called the true mind, or are there different terms?

The answer to this is that Buddhism and Zen give it different names. The bodhisattva precepts of Buddhism call it the mind ground, because it produces all virtues. *Transcendent Wisdom* scriptures call it awakening, because awareness is its essence. The *Flower Ornament Scripture* defines it as the universe of realities, because it pervades and contains all. The *Diamond Scripture* calls it that which realizes suchness, because it comes from nowhere. *Transcendent Wisdom* scriptures call it nirvana, because it is the resort of all sages. The *Golden Light Scripture* calls it being-as-is, because it is eternally unchanging. The *Pure Name Scripture* calls it the spiritual body, because experience and manifestation depend on it. The *Treatise on Awakening of Faith* calls it true suchness, because it is unborn and unperishing. The *Nirvana Scripture* calls it Buddha-nature, because it is the substance of the three bodies of Buddha. The *Scripture of Complete Enlightenment* calls it total command, because it emanates virtuous qualities. The *Scripture of the Lion's Roar of Queen Shrimala* calls it the matrix of realization of suchness, because it conceals and contains. The *Scripture of Perfect Doctrine* calls it complete awareness, because it breaks through darkness, shining alone. So Zen master Yung-ming's *Secret of Mind Alone* says, "One reality has a thousand names, designated according to conditions; they are all in the scriptures and treatises, too numerous to cite them all."

Now that we know about Buddhism, it may be asked, what about Zen? To this it may be replied that Zen stops all naming and verbalizing. If even one name is not established, how could there be many names? And yet, when responding to feelings and adapting to potentials, there are indeed many names. Sometimes it is called the self, because it is the basic essence of a living being. Sometimes it is called the true eye, because it mirrors all appearances. Sometimes it is called the wondrous mind, because its open awareness shines serenely. Sometimes it is called the host or master, because it has been carrying the burden all along. Sometimes it is called the bottomless bowl, because of living life wherever one may be. Sometimes it is called the stringless harp, because its melody is beyond the present. Sometimes it is called the inexhaustible lamp, because its illumination breaks through deluded feelings. Sometimes it is called the rootless tree, because the root and stem are firm and strong. Sometimes it is called a razor-sharp sword, because it cuts through senses and objects. Sometimes it is called the land of effortlessness, because the ocean is peaceful and the rivers clear. Sometimes it is called the pearl of the sage, because it rescues the poor and the destitute. Sometimes it is called the keyless lock, because it locks up the six senses. It is also called the clay ox, the wood horse, the mind source, the mind seal, the mind mirror, the mind moon, the mind pearl. There are too many different names to note them all. If you arrive at the true mind, all names are clear; if you are ignorant of this true mind, all names hang you up. Therefore you had best be very careful about the true mind.

Substance

One of the most basic distinctions conceived in east Asian thinking is drawn between substance and function. This distinction, furthermore, is not made as a philosophical abstraction but as a pragmatic framework of perception, understanding, and action. Chinul makes this distinction in reference to the true mind in order to help the reader avoid mistaking a product of the mind, such as an idea or a feeling, with the essential nature of mind itself. This is critical for the experiential realization of kensho.

When Zen texts speak of emptiness, voidness, equanimity, purity, or the spacelike nature of mind, it is this aspect of "substance" to which they refer. The emptiness, voidness, equanimity, purity, and spacelike quality refer to the nonconceptual, nonemotional nature of the experience of the substance or "body" of the true mind.

Thus the descriptions of the substance of true mind are some-

7

thing like parameters of attention, guidelines for the focus of attention needed for the Zen experience.

The Subtle Substance of the True Mind

Now that we know the names of the true mind, what about its substance? The *Scripture of Radiant Wisdom* says, "Wisdom has no form, no sign of origination or extinction." The *Treatise on Awakening of Faith* says, "The substance of true suchness is neither more nor less in ordinary people, learners, those awakened to conditionality, enlightening beings, and the Buddhas. It was not originated in the past and will not perish in the future; it is ultimately eternal. It has always been inherently replete with all effective qualities."

According to this scripture and treatise, the basic substance of the true mind transcends causality and pervades time. It is neither profane nor sacred; it has no oppositions. Like space itself, it is omnipresent; its subtle substance is stable and utterly peaceful, beyond all conceptual elaboration. It is unoriginated, imperishable, neither existent nor nonexistent. It is unmoving, unstirring, profoundly still and eternal.

This is called the inner host that has always been there, or the person before the prehistoric Buddhas, or the self before the aeon of emptiness. Uniformly equanimous, it is totally flawless and unblemished. All things, pure and impure—mountains, rivers, earth, grasses, trees, forests, all forms and appearances—all come forth from this. Therefore the *Scripture of Complete Enlightenment* says, "The supreme regent of Truth has a method of mental command called complete awareness, which emanates all pure suchness, enlightenment, nirvana, and the ways of transcendence, teaching them to enlightening beings."

Kuei-feng said, "The mind is immaterial and immaculate, with radiant awareness. Neither coming nor going, it pervades all time; neither inside nor outside, it permeates all space. Unperishing and unoriginated, it cannot be harmed by material elements; beyond nature and appearances, it cannot be blinded by sense objects."

Therefore Yung-ming's *Secret of Mind Alone* says, "This mind encompasses all wonders and all perceptions, being monarch of all truths; it is the refuge of all ways of freedom and all types of potential, being mother of all sages." Uniquely noble, peerless, the real source of enlightenment, it is the true essence of the teachings. Trust in it, and the enlightening beings of all times are fellow students, all studying this mind. The Buddhas of all times have the same realization, all realizing this mind; what the teachings of the whole canon bring out is this mind. What the confusions of all people confuse is this mind; when practitioners awaken understanding, what they awaken understanding of is this mind. What all the Zen masters communicate is this mind; what all Zen seekers are seeking is this mind.

When you arrive at this mind, it is everywhere; everything reveals it all. As long as you are confused about this mind, you are deluded everywhere and always crazed. This substance is the Buddha-nature inherent in everyone, the root source of the evolution of all worlds.

This is why Buddha was silent on Vulture Peak, why Subhuti forgot words on a crag, why Bodhidharma gazed like a wall at Shaolin, why Vimalakirti clammed up at Vaisali—all of them were bringing to light the subtle substance of mind. So those who are entering into Zen should first get to know this mind substance.

Function

A common fallacy about Zen, both in the East and in the West, is that it involves destruction of the capacity of thought and reason. While Zen does involve detachment from thoughts, this is not an end but a means, and does not include destruction or compromise of reason. Detachment from thoughts is a means of undermining automatic mental habits and compulsive subjective rationalization. It is not for blanking the mind or diminishing the intelligence.

Experiential realization of the true mind does not nullify its abilities but, rather, liberates them. Intimacy with the true mind opens up possibilities of perception, thought, and feeling in new dimensions, more accurately and more comprehensively than ever before, more perfectly and more completely than what is facilitated by rigidly held conventions and subjective proclivities.

Subtle Function of the True Mind

Now that we know the subtle substance, what is its subtle function? An ancient said, "When the wind blows, mind stirs the trees; when clouds appear, nature raises dust. If you clarify the phenomena of the present day, you obscure the original human being." This is the subtle substance producing function.

The subtle substance of the true mind is basically immovable, calm and quiet, real and eternal. When subtle function appears from the true substance, you find the subtlety along with the flow. Therefore a verse by a master teacher says, "Mind operates to adapt to all situations; the locus of its operation is truly recondite. If you can recognize essential nature while going along with the flow, there is neither rejoicing nor sorrow."

So all activities at all times are manifestations of the subtle function of the true mind. Ordinary people who are deluded just think they are dressing when they dress, and just think they are eating when they eat; in all their business they just operate in conformity to appearances. That is why "it is in their daily activities without their being aware of it; it is right before their eyes without their knowing it."

Thus a master teacher said, "In the womb, it is called a spirit; in the world, it is called a person. In the eyes it sees, in the ears it hears, in the nose it smells, in the mouth it talks, in the hands it grips, in the feet it walks. It appears everywhere, encompassing the universe, yet is concentrated in a single atom." Those who know this call it Buddha-nature; those who do not know it call it soul.

So one master flipped a bamboo stick, another drew a bow, another wielded a forked stick, another raised a finger, another hit the ground; all of them were bringing this great function to light. If you do not confuse it in the course of everyday activities, you will naturally be free and unimpeded.

Relationship between Substance and Function

Substance and function of true mind are differentiated for expedient reasons, in order to avoid mistaking subjective feelings for true substance and conditioned thoughts for true function. If substance and function were to remain separate, however, the individual would be split between stillness and activity, with no way to integrate them.

In order to establish experiential unity without losing the pragmatic utility of the distinction between substance and function, Chinul demonstrates how the substance and function of the true mind can be seen as one yet different, different yet one, without this causing either logical or practical confusion.

Unity and Difference of Substance and Function of the True Mind

It may be asked whether the substance and function of the true mind are one or different. In terms of characteristics, they are not one; in terms of essence, they are not different. Therefore the substance and function are not one and not different.

How do we know? Let's try to discuss it. The subtle substance is immutable, beyond all oppositions, apart from all appearances; without arriving at its essence and actually experiencing it, no one can fathom its principle. Subtle function responds to all types according to conditions, creating illusory appearances, seeming to have forms.

From this perspective, one has form and the other is formless, so they are not one and the same.

And yet, function emerges from substance, function is not apart from substance. Substance is what produces function, so substance is not apart from function. From this perspective, in principle they are indivisible, so they are not different.

It is like water having wetness for its substance, because substance has no motion; waves are characterized by movement, because they are aroused by the wind. Wetness is substance, waves are function; one is in movement and the other unmoving, so they are not one and the same. Nevertheless, there is no water outside of waves, and there are no waves outside of water; the nature of wetness is one, so they are not different. The oneness and difference of substance and function can be recognized by analogy.

Confusion

Although the true mind is universal in principle, in practice there are differences in mentalities, according to conditioning. Confusing temporary reflections with the nature of mind itself is delusion; this prevents the individual from realizing the true mind as it is. That does not mean, however, that the true mind is not there, for confusion itself could not then exist.

The True Mind in Confusion

It may be asked, since the substance and function of the true mind are inherent in everyone, then why are sages and ordinary people not the same? The answer is that the true mind is basically the same in sages and ordinary people, but ordinary people perceive things in an arbitrary, subjective way, losing the inherently pure essence and thus being obstructed by this. That is why the true mind cannot become manifest, but just remains like the shadow of a tree at night, or a subterranean spring—it is there, but is simply not perceived.

Therefore a scripture says, "Just as a clear jewel reflects all colors, so the ignorant think it is colored, in the same way the pure essence of complete awareness manifests in the body and mind according to individual type, and the ignorant say that pure complete awareness really has such physical and mental identities."

The *Discourses of Chao* says, "In the universe, within time and space, there is a treasure, hidden in the mountain of form." This refers to the true mind under wraps. Tz'u-en also says, "The body of reality is inherent, common to all Buddhas; ordinary people have it but do not realize it, because it is covered by illusions. Because passions wrap it up, it gets the name of the mine of realization of suchness.

Master P'ei said, "Those who are completely aware all day yet never completely aware of it are ordinary people." So we know that the true mind is unstained by worldly troubles, just as a white jade will not change color when tossed into mud.

Stopping Delusion

Zen texts describe many methods for stopping delusion and con-fusion in order to arrive at the true mind. Chinul calls the basis of these methods "mindlessness" in conformity with Zen custom, explaining that this does not mean unconsciousness. It should also be explained that "mindlessness" does not mean ignorance or witlessness, as some moderns would seem to suggest in their writings and their behavior; nor does it mean thoughtlessness and irrationality.

Chinul presents ten basic exercises in mindlessness, extracted from traditional Zen teachings. There are also hundreds of Zen koans representing these ten basic exercises, of which Chinul gives a few examples.

According to Chinul, it is not necessary to practice all ten methods; any one of them will lead to realization of the true mind, provided it is the one that works for the individual concerned. Chinul recommends practicing whichever one you have affinity with, but that requires "tasting" them all to know, and it requires the ability to distinguish affinity from attraction.

For example, an introverted person might feel attracted to an exercise involving "disappearance of objects," but affinity in the Zen sense is based on need, not desire. Oblivion to objects is usually about the last thing an excessively introverted person needs. Conversely, an unreflective extrovert might be attracted only to exercises involving communion with the world at large, whereas such an approach may well just exaggerate this particular individual's imbalance.

Thus when Chinul speaks of affinity according to inclination, this does not mean indulgence in subjective wishes but, rather, objectively understanding your own inclinations to see what you actually need in order to attain the Zen "mindlessness," or non-subjective true mind.

Chinul concludes this essay by noting that these exercises do not involve deliberate effort. He calls this "effortless work." An ancient proverb says, "If you hurry, you don't succeed." This principle, that trying too hard retards progress, is also clearly articulated in Taoism. Medieval and latter-day Zen cults have too often ignored this principle in favor of obsession and excess.

The True Mind Stops Delusion

It may be asked, if we are ordinary people as long as the true mind is in delusion, how can we get it out of delusion to attain enlightenment? To answer this, let us cite an ancient saying: "When the deluded mind is nowhere, this is enlightenment." Scripture says, "People's illusory body perishes, so the illusory mind also perishes. Because the illusory mind perishes, illusory objects also perish. Because illusory objects perish, illusory perishing perishes. Because illusory perishing perishes, that which is not illusory does not perish. It is like polishing a mirror; when the dirt is gone, the clarity appears." Yung-chia also said, "Mind is the sense, phenomena are the object; both are like flaws in a mirror. When the flaws and dirt are gone, only then does the light show; when mind and phenomena are both forgotten, essential nature is real." This refers to getting out of delusion and attaining reality.

Chuang-tzu said, "The mind is hotter than fire, colder than ice; it is so fast that it covers all beyond the four seas in the moment of a nod. When at rest, it is profoundly calm, its action gushes forth from nature; such is the human mind." This is Taoist master Chuang-tzu's earlier explanation of the intractability of the human mind; it may be asked, what means does Zen use to quell the errant mind?

The answer to this is that we use the means of no mind to quell the errant mind.

It may be asked, if people are mindless, they are the same as plants and trees; let us have some expedient method of applying the teaching of mindlessness.

To this it may be replied that when we speak of mindlessness we do not mean mindlessness as absence of the substance of mind; when there are no things on the mind, *that* is called mindlessness. It is like an empty jar being called an empty jar because it has nothing in it, not because the substance of the jar itself isn't there. So a master teacher said, "Just have no things in your mind and no mind in things; you will naturally be empty and spiritual, serene and sublime." This is the essence of mind; based on this, the pragmatic meaning of mindlessness is that there is no deluded errant mind, not that there is no subtle function of true mind.

Teachers of the past have given various different kinds of explanations of doing exercises in mindlessness. Now let us sum up the main principles in brief elucidations of ten kinds.

1. *Alert Observation.* When doing the inner work, you always cut off thoughts and prevent thoughts from arising. The instant a thought arises, you immediately break through it by awakeness. When errant thoughts are broken through by awakeness, following

thoughts do not arise; then you no longer need this wakening knowledge. When confusion and awakening are both forgotten, this is called mindlessness. Therefore a master teacher said, "Do not fear thoughts' arising; just be wary of being slow to become aware of it." There is also a verse that says, "You do not need to seek reality, just stop entertaining views and opinions." This is working on stopping illusion by alert observation.

2. *Cessation.* When you work, do not think of good or bad. When the mind is aroused, stop right away; when you encounter objects, cease and desist. An ancient said, "Be like a piece of white silk; be cool; be like the censer in an abandoned temple." Then you are free from vagueness and detached from false discrimination. Be like an ignoramus or a dunce, and then you will attain some accord. This is working on stopping illusion by putting the mind to rest.

3. *Mind Disappears While Objects Remain.* When you work, stop all random thoughts. Paying no attention to external objects, you just stop your own mind. Once the errant mind has stopped, what is the harm if there are objects there? This is the ancient teaching of "taking away the subject but not the objects." Thus there is a saying, "Here there is fragrant grass, but no old friends in the city." Also, lay master P'ang said, "Just have no mind on anything, and what does it matter if everything surrounds you?" This is working on stopping delusion by having mind disappear while letting objects remain.

4. *Objects Disappear While Mind Remains.* When you work, you view all objects, both internal and external, as totally null and void, just keeping one mind alone and independent. Thus an ancient said, "Don't be a partner to myriad things, don't relate to the sense data." If mind sticks to objects, the mind is confused; now if there are no objects, what confusion can there be? Then the true mind shines alone, not obstructed from the Way. This is what an ancient master teacher called removing objects but not the subject. Thus it is said, "Going into the garden, you find the flowers have already fallen; but horses and carriages still fill the place." It is also said, "Three thousand warriors—where are they now? I only consider Chuang-tzu able

to establish great peace." This is working on stopping delusion by letting objects disappear while mind remains.

5. *Mind and Objects Both Disappear.* When you work, first you make external objects empty and silent, then you extinguish your inner mind. Since inner mind and outer objects are both silent, ultimately where can confusion come from? Therefore an ancient master said, "There are no walls in the ten directions, no gates in the four quarters." You are clean and naked, bare and untrammeled. This is the ancient masters' teaching of simultaneously removing both subject and object. There is a saying in reference to this that goes, "The clouds have dispersed, the water run off; profoundly silent, heaven and earth are empty." There is also a saying, "When the herder and the ox have both disappeared, this is precisely when the moon is bright and clear." This is working on stopping delusion by making mind and objects both disappear.

6. *Leaving Mind and Objects There.* When you work, mind abides in the normal state of mind, objects abide in the normal state of objects. Whenever mind and objects face each other, mind does not grasp objects and objects do not rule the mind; neither actually reaches the other, so confused thoughts naturally do not arise, and there is no hindrance to the Way. Therefore scripture says, "These phenomena abide in the normal state of phenomena; the characteristics of the world are always there." This is the teaching of removing neither subject nor object, of which it is said, "When the single moon rises over the ocean, how many people go upstairs to see it!" It is also said, "Amid the myriad mountain flowers, the wanderer does not know the way back." This is working on extinguishing delusion while leaving objects and mind there.

7. *Total Substance, Inside and Out.* When you work, you realize that all things—the mountains, rivers, earth, sun, moon, stars, and planets, the inner body and outer world—are the same as the substance of the true mind. Profoundly calm, open and clear, there is not the slightest difference. The whole universe becomes one; then where do you find the confused mind? Thus dharma master Seng Chao said, "Heaven, earth, and I have the same root; all things and I

are the same body." This is working on destroying delusion by the total substance of inside and outside.

8. *Total Function, Inner and Outer.* When you work, you view all things, internal and external—body, mind, and the material world, including all doings and activities—as marvelous functions of the true mind. The instant they arise, all thoughts in the mind are manifestations of miraculous function. Since it is all miraculous function, where can the confused mind rest? Therefore Yung-chia said, "The real nature of ignorance is Buddha-nature; the illusory empty body is the body of reality." In Master Pao-chih's Twelve Hour Verses, he wrote, "At dawn, wild potential hides within a wayfarer's body; sitting, lying down, he doesn't know it's originally the Way. In such a hurry, he feels bitter pain." This is working on stopping delusion by total inner and outer function.

9. *Substance Identical to Function.* When you work, even though you subtly merge with reality and there is uniform emptiness and silence, nevertheless effective luminosity is concealed therein, so the substance is identical to the function. Within effective luminosity, there is concealed empty silence, so the function is identical to the substance. Therefore Yung-chia said, "Alert tranquillity is right, indifferent tranquillity is wrong." Since indifference is not allowed in tranquillity, and random thoughts are not used in alertness, where can any confused mind come from? This is working on destroying delusion by the identity of substance and function.

10. *Passing Through and Beyond Substance and Function.* When you work, you do not divide inside from outside, and do not distinguish east, west, south, north: you take the four quarters and eight directions and just make it all into one big door of liberation. In this perfect roundness, substance and function are not divided. There is not the slightest leak, the whole being is one. Where can confusion arise? An ancient said, "The whole being is seamless; above and below, all is one sphere." This is working on destroying delusion by passing through and beyond substance and function.

It is not necessary to use all of these ten methods of doing the work; just master one method, and when the work is accomplished, delusion will spontaneously disappear and the true mind will thereupon emerge. Practice whatever method you have affinity with, according to your faculties and existing inclinations.

This work is effortless work; it is not deliberate effort. I have explained the most about these methods of stopping the false mind because this is what is most essential.

Posture

Long hours of discomfort in cross-legged sitting is one of the popular images of Zen promoted by latter-day cult impresarios. The pain of an unfamiliar posture is even touted by some preachers as itself an ingredient of Zen. This is very convenient for "teachers" who prefer to keep their "disciples" preoccupied, but this is not a traditional teaching, and Chinul clearly demonstrates its fallacy.

The point of sitting to meditate, according to traditional authorities, is because of stability and ease, not discomfort and pain. Chinul cites directions for meditation practice from classical sources, which do not recommend self-torture. It will also be noticed that these directions do not call for sitting in groups, as so often recommended by cultists as a substitute for self-discipline. The connection that the meditator is to maintain is not with a limited self-selected, self-centered group of devotees but with all people, all beings, and Life at large.

The True Mind and the Four Postures

It may be asked whether the cessation of delusion is only practiced while sitting, or whether it also extends to walking, standing, and so on. The answer to this is that while scriptures and treatises mostly speak of sitting practice, that is because it is easy to accomplish that way; they also include walking, standing, and so on, because a gradual development takes place.

The *Treatise on Awakening of Faith* says, "If you are going to practice cessation, stay in a quiet place, sit up straight, and direct your attention so that it does not rest on the breathing, or on the body, or on space, or on earth, water, fire, or air, or on any perception or cognition; getting rid of all mental images as they come to mind, also dismiss the thought of getting rid of anything. Because all things originally have no mental images, in each instant of awareness, they are unborn and unperishing. Moreover, you cannot mindfully get rid of mind after each time you think of objects outside of mind; if the mind races off in distraction, then gather it back into true mindfulness.

"This true mindfulness is knowing there is only mind, no external objects; once you revert to this mind, it has no form of its own. It is ungraspable, moment to moment.

"When you rise from sitting, in your comings and goings and various activities, at all times be constantly mindful of expedient technique, being observant under all conditions; after long practice of this, it will become unopposed and fully mature, so the mind will attain stabilization. By mental stability, you gradually become powerful and sharp, able to enter absorption in true suchness wherever you are. Profoundly subduing psychological afflictions, the mind of faith grows, rapidly developing without regression. Just get rid of doubt, confusion, distrust, slander, evildoing, bad habits, conceit, and sloth; for such people cannot gain access." Based on this, all four postures—sitting, standing, walking, reclining—will work.

The *Scripture of Complete Enlightenment* says, "First practice cessation as the Buddha taught; keeping the precepts for the security of the community, sit peacefully in a quiet room." This is elementary practice; Yung-chia said, "Meditating, whether walking or sitting, whether speaking or silent, active or still, your being is at peace."

To sum up this discussion on the power of exercises, even sitting cannot stop the mind; how can walking, standing, and so on access the Way? If your practical application reaches whole maturity, even if a thousand sages came forth you would not be startled, and a thou-

sand monsters couldn't turn your head; then how could you be unable to do the work while walking, standing, or sitting?

Suppose someone has a grudge against another and wants to get
revenge. No matter what he is doing, he cannot forget his vendetta.
The same is true when someone wants to make love to another. Since
things in consciousness, like emotions, can be contained in the conscious mind, how could it be doubted that this mindless work can be
constantly present in all four postures? The only thing to fear is not
trusting and not practicing; if you practice and trust, then the Way
will not be lost whatever your posture.

Location

Once the concept of the true mind is introduced, there is a ten-
dency to seek the true mind conceptually. The true mind is obscured by imaginative seeking, yet even with this rational
understanding, the seeking mind tends to seek in terms familiar
to it, in concepts to which the temporal consciousness has been
habituated. Even trying to go beyond this, conditioned consciousness will try to assign the true mind to a hypothetical realm
apart; this is falsehood and illusion. Chinul stresses the fact that
the substance of true mind is actually everywhere, even if unper-
ceived, while its function becomes manifest unpredictably, according to circumstances. This point of emphasis is presented to
halt the arbitrary seeking mind.

Where the True Mind Is

It may be asked, if the true mind appears when the false mind is
stopped, then where are the substance and function of the true mind
right now? The answer is that the subtle substance of the true mind
is everywhere; as Yung-chia said, "There is constant peace wherever
you are; if you seek it, I know you can't see." A scripture says, "It is

spacious, immutable; there is no origination or extinction in the matrix of realization of suchness." Fa-yen said, "Every place is the road of enlightenment, everywhere is the forest of virtues." This is where the substance is.

As for the subtle function of the true mind, it manifests with sensitive adaptivity; it is like a valley echoing a call. Fa-teng said, "Response forever intact, it is clearly there before your eyes; a fleck of cloud arises in an evening valley, a lone crane descends in the distant sky."

This is why Yuan Hua-yen of Wei-fu said, "Buddhism is in daily activities; it is in walking, standing, sitting, and reclining; it is in eating and drinking; it is in speaking and conversing. But if what you do excites your mind and stirs your thoughts, then it isn't right."

So we know that the substance is everywhere, and can produce function anywhere. It is just that the subtle function is indefinite because the presence or absence of causal conditions is indefinite; it is not that there is no subtle function.

If people cultivating mind want to enter the ocean of effortlessness and cross over all births and deaths, do not be confused about where the substance and function are.

Escaping Death

Eastern Buddhists use the term *samsara*, translated into Chinese as "birth and death," in many ways. Sometimes it refers to mundane life in general, particularly in respect to repeating habitual patterns. In its most immediate sense, "birth and death" refers to the stream of passing thoughts that occupy and affect our surface consciousness.

The True Mind Escapes Death

It may be asked: though they say people who see essential nature escape birth and death, nevertheless the masters of the past, who all

saw essential nature, all were born and did die; and people who practice the Way today obviously have birth and death—how can we
speak of escaping birth and death?

The answer to this is that birth and death are fundamentally nonexistent; they are falsely construed to exist. It is like a man with
diseased eyes seeing flowers in the sky; if someone without this disease says there are no flowers in the sky, the afflicted man won't
believe it. Only when the eye disease is gone, whereupon the flowers
in the sky disappear of themselves, will he believe the flowers do not
exist.

Even if the flowers have not disappeared, they are still void. It's
just that the diseased one misconstrues them to be flowers; they do
not really exist. This is like a man who misperceives birth and death
as existing being told by someone free of birth and death that there
is fundamentally no birth and death. If the man's delusions stop one
day, birth and death will spontaneously disappear; only then will he
realize that birth and death are fundamentally nonexistent. Yet even
while birth and death have not disappeared, they are still not really
existent; they exist because of misapprehension.

Scripture says, "The various delusions into which people have
fallen since time immemorial are like the way the four directions
differ to someone who is lost. They misapprehend physical elements
as the forms of their own bodies, and take reflections of objects of
the six senses as the forms of their own minds. That is like people
with diseased eyes seeing flowers in the sky. . . . When unreal flowers
in the sky disappear in space, they cannot be said to have a definite
place of disappearance, because they have no place of origin. In the
same way, people misperceive birth and death where there is no origination; that is why they say there is routine birth and death."

Based on this passage of scripture, we realize that when we attain
enlightenment and completely awaken the true mind, there is basically no birth and death. If you know there is no birth and death, yet
you cannot escape birth and death, it is because your inner work is
insufficient. Thus in the teachings it says that a woman asked Manjushri, "Clearly life is an unborn phenomenon; why are we swept

along by birth and death?" Manjushri said, "Because of insufficiency of strength." Someone asked Hsiu-shan the same question; he responded, "Bamboo shoots eventually become bamboo, but can they be used for twine right now?"

So, knowing there is no birth and death is not as good as comprehending there is no birth and death. Comprehending there is no birth and death is not as good as realizing there is no birth and death. Realizing there is no birth and death is not as good as making use of freedom from birth and death.

People today do not even know there is no birth and death, much less comprehend there is no birth and death, realize there is no birth and death, and make use of freedom from birth and death. So if people who recognize birth and death do not believe there is no birth or death, isn't that fitting?

Direct and Auxiliary Methods

When Buddhist schools began to specialize in certain practices and procedures, it was customary to classify methods into principal and auxiliary. Generally speaking, spiritual exercises given main emphasis in a particular speciality are called principal, while exercises supporting the main focus are called auxiliary. Sometimes all methods other than the given specialization are referred to as auxiliary practices.

In the present case, Chinul considers "the work of mindlessness" to be the main, or "direct" method, while doing good deeds in general is considered auxiliary. Chinul likens the work of mindlessness to cleaning a dusty mirror, with goodness being like a polishing agent assisting in the operation.

True Mind, Direct and Auxiliary Methods

It may be asked, if we stop delusion, the true mind appears, as already explained, but while delusion has not stopped, do we just stop mind wandering and work on mindlessness, or are there other methods of quelling delusion?

The answer to this is that direct and auxiliary methods are not the same. Using the true mind to stop delusion is considered direct, while practicing all sorts of goodness is considered auxiliary. It is like polishing a dusty mirror; you may wipe it by hand, but you need to use a polishing agent before the shine of the mirror appears. The dust on the mirror stands for psychological afflictions, the work of the hand stands for the work of mindlessness, the polishing agent stands for virtues, and the shine of the mirror stands for the true mind.

The *Treatise on Awakening of Faith* says, "What kind of mentality is developed by perfection of faith? It is threefold. For one thing, it is a straightforward mentality, because of direct attention on the reality of true suchness. Second, it is a profound mentality, because it puts together all good conduct. Third, it is a very compassionate mentality, desiring to free all beings from misery.

Question: It has been explained that the cosmos of realities is a unity, and the substance of Buddhahood has no duality. Why not just keep true suchness in mind? Why seek to practice good deeds?

Answer: A jewel may be essentially pure, but it is defiled by the ore; if people only think of the essence of the jewel and do not methodically polish it, the jewel will never get cleaned. The reality of true suchness is essentially open and pure, but there is defilement by countless psychological afflictions. Even if people are mindful of true suchness, they will never attain it purely unless they use expedient means to cultivate this. Because defilement is infinite and extends to all things, we cultivate all kinds of good deeds as remedies. Because if people practice all kinds of good deeds, they will naturally wind up in accord with the reality of true suchness.

Based on this treatment of the subject, stopping the deluded mind is direct, cultivating good qualities is auxiliary. When you cultivate goodness, if you are in tune with mindlessness you do not grasp cause and effect. If you grasp cause and effect, then you get caught up in human and heavenly rewards experienced by ordinary mortals, so it is impossible to witness true suchness and you do not escape birth and death. If you tune in to mindlessness, this is the essential technique for witnessing true suchness and escaping birth and death, and you simultaneously attain great blessings.

The *Scripture on Adamantine Wisdom* says, "When enlightening beings give without dwelling on appearances, the blessings are inconceivable." Now we see worldly people who have studied some Zen presume upon natural reality as soon as they learn there is an intrinsic Buddha-nature, and do not cultivate virtues. Not only do they fail to arrive at the true mind, they also become lazy. They cannot even avoid bad ways, much less escape birth and death. Their view is very mistaken.

Virtues

Clarification of the true mind, described as "mindlessness," does not refer to a state of blankness, indifference, or literal mental voidness, even if some would-be practitioners may give such an impression to outside observers. Clarification allows the inherent "virtues" or qualities and capacities of mind to express themselves in a wholesome and spontaneous way. This natural endowment is contrasted with "virtues" conceptually posited and deliberately cultivated, which can contrarily foster self-absorbtion and conceit.

Virtues of the True Mind

It may be asked: the virtue in mindful cultivation of cause is unquestionable; but where does the virtue in mindless cultivation come from? The answer to this is that mindful cultivation of cause results in artificial effects, whereas mindless cultivation of cause reveals the virtues of essential nature.

These virtues are inherent, but they are not manifest because of being covered by delusion. Now, once delusion is removed, the virtues appear. Therefore Yung-chia said, "The Three Embodiments and Four Knowledges are complete in the substance; the eight liberations and six powers are impressions of basic mind." This refers to the virtues of essential nature inherent in the substance.

An ancient verse says, "If someone sits quietly for a moment, that is better than building countless shrines of jewels. The jewel shrines will ultimately turn into dust, but a moment's pure mind attains true awakening." So we know that the achievement of mindlessness is better than mindfulness.

Shui-liao called on Ancestor Ma and asked, "What is the precise meaning of the coming of living Zen?" In reply, he got kicked over by Ancestor Ma, whereupon he was suddenly enlightened. Getting up, he clapped and said with a laugh, "How wonderful! How marvelous! A hundred thousand meditations and infinite sublime principles are discerned all at once, right at their source, on the tip of a single hair!" Then he paid his respects and left. Based on this example, virtuous qualities do not come from outside but are inherently there.

The fourth patriarch of Zen said to Zen master Lazy Jung, "All the countless facets of the Teaching ultimately refer to the heart; infinite virtues are all in the mind source. All modes of discipline, concentration, and knowledge, all spiritual powers and miraculous projections, are inherent, not apart from your mind." According to the words of the patriarch, the virtues of mindlessness are enormous; it is just that those who are devoted to formal merit do not believe in the merit of mindlessness.

Testing the True Mind

Glimpsing or sensing the clarity of the true mind may awaken the individual to hints of its vast potential, but unless it is tested and tempered in experience and action, the living consciousness of the true mind can hardly be stabilized.

Many people attempt to accomplish stabilization by means of

cloistering and environmental limitation, but the fatal drawbacks of this approach are evident through history. According to a famous teaching story from Zen lore, the second patriarch of Zen in China personally spent thirty years as a laborer after his enlightenment, testing and tuning his mind. Based on this tradition, Chinul gives some precise instructions on testing the mind internally in the process of stabilization.

Testing the Effectiveness of the True Mind

It may be asked, when the true mind becomes manifest, how do we know it is the true mind developed to maturity, free from impediment? The answer to this is that when people learning the Way have already attained manifestation of the true mind but the energy of their habits is not yet gone, their attention may sometimes slip when they are in familiar circumstances.

It is like herding an ox; even though it may be trained to the point where it follows along docilely at the tug of the rope, one still does not dare abandon the whip and the rope. One can only let go when its heart is tame and its step peaceful, such that even when driven into a field of seedlings it does not harm the plants. At this stage, there is no need for the herder's whip and rope; there is naturally no destruction of seedlings.

Similarly, when people on the Way have attained the true mind, first they use effort for a while to preserve and nurture it, for only with great powerful function is it feasible to help others.

When you test the true mind, first pick things you've always liked and imagine from time to time that they are there before you; if you feel revulsion or attraction as before, then the enlightened mind is immature. If you do not conceive any revulsion or attraction, then the enlightened mind is mature.

But even though you attain such maturity, this is still not the stage where you naturally do not produce aversion or attraction. Check your mind again: when you encounter things you dislike or things you like, if you conceive aversion or attraction, this will cause you to grasp those repulsive or attractive objects. If the mind is not aroused, then it is unobstructed, like a white ox on open ground not damaging seedlings.

In ancient times, there were those who scolded the Buddhas and reviled the patriarchs, but they had harmonized with their mind. As for the people we see today who immediately imitate those who scolded the Buddhas and reviled the patriarchs as soon as they go into Zen studies, before they even know how far the journey is, they are way too hasty!

Knowledge

The most subtle barrier to kensho, the basic Zen insight, the obstacle most hard to overcome, is the barrier of knowledge. Transcending this barrier requires experiential distinction between direct perception and conceptual description. When Buddhists speak of the true mind as having no knowledge, the original meaning is that direct perception is veritable, whereas conceptual elaboration is not. Unfortunately, followers of deteriorated Zen, lacking insight, have mistaken ignorance and blindness, sometimes even sheer silliness, for the "no knowledge" of direct perception. Chinul shows how "knowing" and "unknowing" are not opposites in the experience of the awakened.

The True Mind Has No Knowledge

It may be asked, when true mind and false mind face objects, how can you distinguish true and false? The answer to this is that when a false or deluded mind faces objects, it has knowledge; and, knowing of pleasant and unpleasant objects, it conceives greed and hatred. In neutral contexts, it also produces stupidity. Since it produces greed, hatred, and stupidity in its relation to objects, that is sufficient evidence that it is a false mind, a deluded mind.

A Zen patriarch said, "The conflict of opposition and accord is sickness in the mind." So we know that what relates to approval and disapproval is a false mind. As for the true mind, it knows without knowledge. It is different from plants and trees by virtue of its equanimous all-around awareness; it is different from deluded mind because it does not give rise to aversion and attraction. So in face of objects it is open and clear, neither repelled nor attracted; because what knows without knowledge is the true mind.

The *Discourses of Chao* says, "The mind of sages is subtle and has no form, so it cannot be considered existent; yet when applied, it works harder and harder, so it cannot be considered nonexistent. Because it is not existent, it knows yet has no knowledge; because it is not nonexistent, it has no knowledge and yet knows." Here unknowing is identical to knowing, so there is nothing to speak of as different from the mind of sages. But the false, deluded mind clings to existence in the context of existence, and clings to nonexistence in the context of nonexistence; always involved in dualistic extremism, it does not know the Middle Way. Yung-chia said, "If you reject the false mind to grasp real truth, the grasping and rejecting mind creates clever artificialities. The unknowing student basing practice on this has, at a deep level, mistaken a thief for a son."

If it is the true mind, it does not get trapped in either being or nonbeing, even though it may be in being or nonbeing. A Zen patriarch said, "Don't pursue conditions of existence, but don't dwell in acceptance of emptiness; with uniform equanimity, they disappear of themselves." The *Discourses of Chao* says, "Thus sages are not existent in being and not nonexistent in nonbeing. But though they do not grasp being and nonbeing, still they do not abandon being and nonbeing, so they can harmonize their enlightenment with the world, circulating through all ways of life, coming in peace and going serenely, tranquil and uncontrived, yet capable of doing anything." This tells us how sages reach out to help others, circulating through all walks of life to meet and transform people. Even though they come and go, they are not marked by coming and going. A deluded mind is not like this; so a deluded mind is not the same as the true mind.

The true mind is also the normal mind, whereas a false or deluded mind is not normal. It may be asked what the normal mind is. The answer is that everyone has a dot of spiritual luminosity, deep as space itself, present everywhere. It is provisionally called noumenal essence, in contrast to mundane phenomena; it is expediently termed true mind, in contrast to false consciousness. Entirely free of arbitrary conceptualization, it is not blinded by contact with objects; without a single thought of grasping or rejection, it comprehends everything it encounters. It does not change along with myriad objects; even if it attains the marvel along with the flow, it never leaves the profound calm of the immediate. "If you seek it, obviously you don't see." This is the true mind.

It may be asked what it is that we are calling the abnormal mind, the mind that is not normal. The answer is that objects may be sacred and profane, polluted and pure, impermanent and permanent, principle and fact, originated and destroyed, moving and still, coming and going, beautiful and ugly, good and bad, causes and effects. All told, there are countless differences; now I have cited ten oppositions, which I call inconstant objects. When the mind arises and passes away along with these inconstant objects, the mind on inconstant objects is opposite to the normal, constant, true mind; therefore it is called an abnormal, false mind. The true mind is inherently complete and does not produce all sorts of distinctions in pursuit of inconstant objects; thus it is called the normal, true mind.

It may be asked, if the true mind is constant and has no incongruous elements, why did Buddha speak of cause and effect, good and bad, consequence and reward? The answer to this is that the deluded mind pursues all sorts of objects, fails to understand all kinds of situations, and then produces all sorts of states of mind. Buddha explained all sorts of laws of causality to remedy all sorts of deluded mentalities; it was necessary to define causes and effects. In the case of the true mind, it does not pursue all sorts of objects, so it does not produce all sorts of mentalities. Thus the Buddha has not expounded all sorts of teachings for the true mind, what cause or effect is there?

It may be asked if the true mind is normally unborn. The answer is that the true mind acts from time to time, but this is not arousal in pursuit of objects. It is just the play of subtle function, not blind to causality.

Destiny

The freedom of the true mind is sometimes called freedom in life and death, or independence at the shoreline of life and death. The foregoing essays by Chinul are on freedom in life; this last one is on freedom in death. This is the freedom of passing through personal disintegration without trauma, consummating the ultimate freedom in death that one has cultivated in life.

Where the True Mind Goes

It may be asked: people who have not arrived at the true mind create good and bad causes because of ignorance of the true mind; by creating good causes they are reconstituted in good ways, and by creating bad causes they enter into bad ways—there is no doubt about the principle of life being conditioned by actions, but if those who have attained the true mind are emptied of deluded feelings and realize the true mind, there are no good or bad causes—where does the spirit cleave after death?

In response to this I would suggest that the questioner may be thinking it better to have a resort to cleave to than to have no resort, and may be thinking that having no resort after death is like being a vagrant in life, or like being a solitary ghost. It may seem this way, but when you arrive at essential nature it is not.

All living beings form habits of action influenced by subjective feelings and affections based on ignorance of the essence of awareness. These habits of action are the causes of specific life patterns, in which the consequences of good and bad are experienced. For example, if heavenly action is the cause, only heavenly results are obtained; only those states of being consonant with one's habitual actions are accessible. Since it is in accord with one's habits, a consonant state of being is considered pleasant, while inaccessible states are considered unpleasant. Consonant states are regarded as one's own resort, whereas other states are regarded as the resorts of others. Thus there is a false sense of reality, and so there are false causes, and thus false effects. Because there are false effects, there is resorting to them; because of resorting to them, there is distinction of other from self. Because of distinguishing other from self, there is approval and disapproval.

Now, when you arrive at the true mind, you merge with the essence of awareness, which has no birth or destruction, and activate birthless and indestructible subtle function. The subtle substance is truly eternal, fundamentally without origin or destruction; the subtle function, adapting to conditions, seems to have origination and disappearance, but since the function comes from the substance, the function is itself the substance, and cannot have any origination or destruction. When adepts witness the true substance, of what concern are beginnings and endings?

It is like water: Moisture is the substance, waves are the function. There is no origination or destruction in the nature of moisture, so how can the moisture in the waves originate or pass away? Since there can be no waves apart from the nature of moisture, therefore the waves are also unborn and unperishing.

Thus an ancient said, "The whole world is a practitioner's pair of eyes; the whole world is a sanctuary." All of it is the place where those who have awakened to the principle live out their lives. Once you've arrived at the true mind, confused states disappear at once, and the mountains, rivers, and indeed the whole earth, are all the true mind—there can be no resort outside this true mind.

Once there are no deluding causes, whether in the realm of desire, form, or formless abstraction, there will be no deluded ways of behaving as a result. Without results of illusion, what resort can be spoken of? There is no other or self, no object or subject—so how can you approve or disapprove? Then the whole universe is just one true mind; the whole body is animated by it, so there is no special resort.

Also, in the process of didactic manifestation, one is reborn at will, without impediment. Hence the story in *Transmission of the Lamp* where the ministry president En Ts'ao asked Kuei-feng, "Where do enlightened people wind up after death?" Kuei-feng replied, "All beings have the essence of awareness, a spiritual luminosity, no different from that of Buddhas. If you awaken to this essence, it is identical to the body of reality; since it comes from nowhere, how could it end up anywhere? When the spiritual luminosity is not obscured, it is always clearly aware. It comes from nowhere and goes nowhere. Just take empty serenity for your own being, not the physical body; consider the spiritual luminosity to be your own mind, not random thoughts. If random thoughts arise, don't follow them at all—then at the end of your life, compulsive habits cannot bind you: even if there is an intermediate state, you can go wherever you want freely, resorting to celestial or human realms at will." This is where the existing true mind goes after the end of the body.

PART TWO

APPLICATIONS

Zen Master Hakuin

Subtle Confusions

Zen master Hakuin lived in a time when Western science and rationalism were trickling into feudal Japan. Hakuin's works on symbolism reveal how poorly understood classical Buddhist texts were in his time, by adherents of Buddhism themselves as well as by secular scholars then attacking Buddhism for what they imagined to be irrationality.

In his essay "In the Holes of Lotus Threads," Hakuin deals with a mythical story from Buddhist scripture, familiar to Zen Buddhists from the classic *Rinzai-roku,* or Record of Lin-chi, a collection of sayings of one of the great ninth-century Chinese masters. In that Zen classic, the story of a fleeing titan hiding inside lotus fibers with eighty-four thousand cohorts is used to illustrate the principle that extraordinary powers do not amount to enlightenment.

Hakuin goes further, analyzing the story in more detail, probing more deeply into its content and structure. He interprets the battle of the titans and the gods as the resurgence of random mentation after attainment of inner stillness in meditation. The victory of the gods is the overcoming of this disturbance. The concealment of the titans in fine fibers is the retreat of impulses into subtle streams of consciousness hidden in feelings of joyfulness at success.

Finally Hakuin brings up a method of "severing" the "fibers" concealing subtle confusions of thought. This method employs a famous Zen koan, "Does a dog have Buddha-nature? No!" Hakuin says to "gnaw on it vertically and horizontally," meaning to bring it to mind to transcend random thought immediately, and to bring it to mind to sweep away random thought in the course of everyday tasks. "Vertically" refers to the relative being subsumed by the absolute, beyond time; "horizontally" refers to the absolute being revealed in the relative, through time.

This exercise is an elementary Zen practice established for the express purpose of attaining the stage of kensho; it is not a permanent observance. Later in his teaching career Hakuin himself came to prefer the use of the koan "What is the sound of one hand clapping?" Perhaps he foresaw the aberration of people claiming to inherit his lineage who have people repeat, audibly or silently, the nonsense syllable "Mu" to mesmerize themselves under the pretext that this is Zen koan work. No.

In the Holes of Lotus Threads

Zen master Rinzai said, "When the titans fought with the king of gods, on losing the battle he led his eighty-four thousand troops into the holes in lotus threads, where they hid. Unable to attack them there, the king of gods withdrew."

This is a scriptural story. I used to wonder why a titan with such miraculous powers would particularly seek out a lotus thread hole to hide when defeated in battle, whereas it could freely hide anywhere—in the eye of a moth, in the nostril of a mosquito, in an atom, on the tip of a needle. Even if all eighty-four thousand troops were inside a subatomic particle, it would not seem confined; so why especially single out lotus thread holes?

Furthermore, once the king of gods had won, given the great power and legendary swiftness of the gods, what time was there to find a lotus pond, break a lotus stem, extract the threads, and then hide inside them? And even if the titans managed to hide, the perception of the gods takes in the whole universe like a crystal in the palm of the hand—how could anything be overlooked?

What if, furthermore, it were early spring, before the lotus leaves have surfaced—there would be no place to hide. Out of luck, would the titans have wound up staining the weapons of the gods with their blood?

I really wondered about this for a long time, until I recently had an unexpected insight into the matter while meditating. Unable to bear my joy, I wrote it down to pass on to my students.

On reflection, it seems that what this is all about is a subtle scriptural metaphor that has a great deal of benefit for working on the path. Let me try to expound this.

Suppose you are working on the path. As you sit up quietly, your body and mind pass away into quiescence, all things are empty and still. The profound void is like infinite space.

Suddenly feelings and thoughts start arising in confusion, like clouds and fog enfolding the whole sky, like gigantic waves swallowing huge mountains. Valleys roar, mountains snort, odiferous mist spews hailstones, toxic fog encages lightning and thunder.

This is the time when the titan prevails in battle, manifesting a giant body so enormous it makes the ocean seem shallow, and the sky seem narrow. Shaking the precious throne room, it hollers and cries with rage; grabbing the sun and moon, it goes berserk in frustration. The pedestal of spirit is shaken up by this, the heart is rent in pieces.

At this point, if you suddenly wake up and bring the mind to the saying you have been contemplating, or else turn to what is inherent in yourself, that is like pouring a dipperful of cool water into a pot of boiling water. The ocean of essential nature becomes calm; the mind source becomes open and aware.

This is the time when the king of the gods prevails in battle. The four guardian kings take their proper places; all the gods rejoice together. The web of the cosmos has infinite dimensions, each reflecting everything else, with infinite centers and peripheries.

At this time, no trace is left of the eighty-four thousand demon troops; above, below, and all around, they cannot be found, even by psychic powers. Now you jump for joy, thinking everything is settled. What you do not realize is that the demons have gone into these subtle thoughts of joy and are hiding there, completely intact.

What are these subtle thoughts? They are subtle streams of consciousness, confusions of thinking that are hard to cut through. So the titan led his followers into confusions of thinking, as hard to cut through as lotus fibers, and hid there. Once they had hidden in the subtle lotus threads of confusions of thinking, it makes sense that the gods withdrew, unable to attack.

In ancient times, Gyozan asked Isan, "How long have you had no subtle streams of consciousness?" Isan replied, "Seven years." This refers to getting entirely rid of the lotus fibers.

How does one do this? Master teachers have a clever technique that cuts through the subtle roots of birth and death like an enormous sword reaching to the sky, crushing your old nest of deluded feelings like a ten-ton hammer. A seeker asked Joshu, "Does a dog have Buddha-nature?" Joshu said, "No." This story has miraculous effects; students who wish to reach the realm of authentic peace and happiness should be sure to gnaw through this story. Gnaw on it vertically, gnaw on it horizontally, and one day you will gnaw through the root of life, die away, and then come back to life.

All this talk is an embarrassment. I urge you not to wait until you've grown old and tears are streaming down your cheeks.

Lofty Illumination

In an essay entitled "The Wonderfully High Lamp Buddha," Hakuin takes up images from the beloved *Vimalakirti-Nirdesa Sutra*, or *Pure Name Scripture*, one of the classical scriptures most often cited in Zen literature, particularly esteemed by lay Buddhists. These images center on number symbolism, whose values are not commonly made explicit either in Buddhist scriptures themselves or in Zen lore.

The first numerical symbol taken up by Hakuin in this essay is the inconceivable quantity referred to by the term "as many as grains of sand in thirty-six Ganges Rivers." Hakuin interprets the three and the six to stand for what are known in Buddhist psychology as the three subtle and the six coarse manifestations of consciousness.

The three subtle manifestations begin with force of habit (historical, cultural, and personal), which activates a particular subjective mentality, resulting in perception of the world in conformity with the subjective mentality. These three manifestations—habit, subjective activation, and objectivized perception—become in turn the psychological substance of the six coarse manifestations.

Working with the three subtle manifestations, the six coarse manifestations of consciousness begin with subjective cognition, which is based on the third subtle manifestation, the subjective perception of the environment. Cognition is made to seem coherent by continuity, or repetition; this is the second coarse manifestation. This continuity is made into a field of conceptual and emotional clinging, the third coarse manifestation, which is firmed and confirmed by assigning labels, the fourth coarse manifestation. Arbitrary concepts and labels condition confused action, the fifth coarse manifestation, which thus results in frustration, the sixth coarse manifestation.

Now Hakuin interprets the scriptural expression of going beyond as many worlds as grains of sand in thirty-six Ganges Rivers to mean going beyond these three subtle and six coarse manifestations to arrive at the very source of mind.

Hakuin goes on to insist that this is not the final realization of Zen. To make his point, he cites a cluster of scriptural images using the number eighty-four thousand, traditionally said to be the number of afflictions to which human beings may be subject, as well as the number of doctrines and practices by which they are remedied in Buddhism. The intent of Hakuin's symbolic allusion here is to equate things of the world with manifestations of basic awakeness.

The scriptural image of the Buddha as eighty-four thousand leagues tall is subsequently transformed into forty-two thousand leagues, ostensibly being halved. This Hakuin interprets on the basis of the four and the two, which he takes to symbolize the classical principles of the four kinds of committed practice and the two kinds of action. The four commitments are commitment to the liberation of all beings, the end of all afflictions, the learning of all truths, and the fulfillment of complete enlightenment. The two kinds of actions are actions done for oneself and actions done for others.

In the end, Hakuin sums up the overall message of this entire essay with a quote from a famous Tendai Buddhist scholar of old, explaining that "equality without distinction is false equality, and distinction without equality is false distinction."

The Wonderfully High Lamp Buddha

In the sixth book of the *Pure Name Scripture*, on the inconceivable, it says, "Vimalakirti asked Manjushri, 'You have traveled to innumerable lands; what Buddha land has the lion throne made of the finest qualities?'

"Manjushri replied, 'To the east, beyond as many lands as grains of sand in thirty-six Ganges Rivers, is a world called Wonderfully High. The Buddha there is called Wonderfully High Lamp. He is presently existing. That Buddha's body is eighty-four thousand leagues tall.' " And so on.

This is the most subtle metaphor in the scripture; its inner meaning is very profound. It is no wonder that even the ancients sometimes missed the meaning. This is the eye of the teachings and the marrow of this scripture. Focusing on pointing out the profound principle of nonduality, it transcends the realm of conceivability. If students will read it carefully and thoroughly, looking into the reality, it can open up the true eye of universal insight into equality.

Having first read this scripture in youth, I really wondered about it. The scripture says there is a world called Wonderfully High beyond lands as numerous as grains of sand in thirty-six Ganges Rivers. I thought to myself that this is very strange; how many trillions of lands is that? I had heard that the Ganges River is enormous; who knows how many million bushels of sand are in its bed, especially with that sand as fine as flour! It would be hard to count all the grains in even a pail of sand, to say nothing of the grains of sand in the bed of an enormous river like the Ganges! Even ghosts and spirits could not count the sand in one Ganges, let alone two, or as many as thirty-six Ganges Rivers!

Obviously this is an immeasurable amount, an incalculable number; but if it is immeasurable and incalculable, why also specify the number thirty-six? Is this not a useless figure, confusing practitioners?

Manjushri was the teacher of seven Buddhas; would he utter useless words to fool us? Could he have been idly making up fantastic supernumbers, or is there a special profound principle? If there is actually a profound principle, why has no one ever brought it out?

This scripture came into the hands of many very intelligent people since entering China. The translators were also extraordinary; there was Yen Fo-t'iao of the Later Han dynasty, Chih-ch'ien of the Wu, Dharmapala and Chu Shu-lan of the Western Chin, and Hsuan-tsang of the T'ang dynasty. The great teacher Chih-che of the Sui dynasty used to lecture on this scripture every summer, making such an impression that even Indian monks came to listen. In the Eastern Chin dynasty, there was Gitamitra; in the Yao Ch'in dynasty, eight hundred outstanding scholars assembled in the Garden of Freedom. As for Kumarajiva, his learning comprehended the whole canon, his perception emptied all of India. Among his disciples, Tao-sheng and Seng-chao were highly illuminated, while Seng-jui and Seng-jung were vastly accomplished. When it came to the principles in the scripture, nothing escaped them; and yet they did not decipher this hidden message. Why?

Even the great master Ch'ang-shui of the Sung dynasty made only a brief comment, elucidating it, writing, "The height of the Buddha's body being eighty-four thousand leagues represents the complete body of reward composed of eighty-four thousand perfections. The height of his throne being eighty-four thousand leagues represents eighty-four thousand aspects of fearlessness realized through emptiness." In my opinion, this explanation is not completely apt.

The book on the inconceivable is the key of the scripture; and the talk of grains of sand in thirty-six Ganges Rivers is the lifeline of the scripture. I always felt like I had something stuck in my teeth, wondering about this for a long time. Recently in meditation, however, I suddenly uncovered the subtle mystery of the scripture, which now appeared before me clearly, to my measureless joy. Come morning, I called my students and told them about it, but there were still those who were as though deaf and dumb, so I have written it down to hand it on, only hoping that you will be as joyful as I am.

If people will look carefully, reading this humble analysis thoroughly, they will surely attain great joy. Once they have experienced this joy, then many hidden subtleties in the *Pure Name Scripture* will become obvious. So don't insist on trashing my poor analysis; I will try to explain this even if others say old Hakuin is chewing food for babies.

If you want to comprehend the meaning here, first you must apply a blade to the field of the storage consciousness. Once you have applied a blade, you will see the Buddha Wonderfully High Lamp King; otherwise, you will never be able to attain resolution all your life.

In the expression "beyond as many lands as grains of sand in thirty-six Ganges Rivers," the word *beyond* is the same as "pass over" used in the term for the six ways of transcendence, or six perfections; *pass over* means "become liberated," and has the meaning of transcending, going beyond. The number thirty-six refers to the three subtle and the six coarse manifestations in the field of the storage consciousness.

What are the three subtle manifestations? The manifestation of historical influences, the manifestation of active arousal, and the manifestation of appearances. These are phenomena presented by the storage consciousness; when you understand them, they are like flowers in the sky.

What about the six coarse manifestations? They are the manifestations of cognition, continuity, clinging, assigning labels, acting compulsively, and suffering through bondage to compulsive action. These are phenomena in the intellectual consciousness; and when you understand them, they are like flowers in the sky.

If a practitioner seeks single-mindedly in concentration, then emotional thoughts will gradually fade away, and one will gradually go back into one's own mind source. This is expressed as "to the east." The eastern direction is associated with thunder and wood, and the season of spring. It is the direction associated with the beginnings of things, so it is called the root of all things.

The meaning of the cognitive and intellectual consciousnesses being gathered back into the basic storage consciousness is clear.

Once the cognitive consciousness looks back into the inherent substance of the storage consciousness itself, you immediately go beyond the boundaries of the three subtle and the six coarse manifestations. Conceptualization stops, emotional thought disappears, and there is utter tranquillity, without a spot of trouble. This is going back into the mind source, profoundly still, the unmoving, unstirring matrix of realization of suchness. That is the meaning of the scripture's statement "Beyond as many worlds as grains of sand in thirty-six Ganges Rivers is a world called Wonderfully High."

This is what people everywhere often mistakenly refer to as the home of the self, the inherent perfect Buddha-mind. What they do not realize is that this is what Ch'ang-sha called the major sign of the circular routine that has gone on since the beginning of time; and it is the "black pit" that Rinzai feared. True practitioners of the Way do not consider reaching this to be enlightenment; they do not consider this enough. If they proceed directly ahead without retreating, before long a certain potential will awaken.

This is called the time when a blade is brought down in the field of the storage consciousness. Who would have anticipated that the storage consciousness now turns into universal mirrorlike cognition, the intellectual consciousness becomes cognition of equality, the cognitive consciousness becomes observant cognition, while the eyes and other basic sense consciousnesses become the cognition to accomplish tasks. Then for the first time you will really believe that the three bodies and the four cognitions of Buddhas are complete within your being. How could the fruits of social virtues or ecstatic states compare to this?

At this time, the grasses, trees, and land, animate and inanimate beings, heavens and hells, Buddha-realms and demon clans, are all a single spiritual light in the universal mirroring cognition. If this is not the Wonderfully High Lamp King Buddha, what is it?

When the light of the Lamp King Buddha shines, the eighty-four thousand pains of impassioned actions are themselves the auspicious marks and embellishments of the Lamp King Buddha. Now the jewel throne is also eighty-four thousand leagues tall, the world is also eighty-four thousand leagues in size, the white hair between the Buddha's eyes is also eighty-four thousand leagues in size, and the pile of offerings is also eighty-four thousand leagues high.

Question: I can accept that in the universal mirroring cognition, passions and enlightenment, pure realms and defiled lands, are one single embodiment of Buddha; but why just hold to the eighty-four thousand passions as the embodiment of Buddha?

Answer: The embodiment of Buddha is most beautiful, while passions are most ugly. The main point of this scripture is the principle of nonduality, revealing insight into equality. Therefore it uses the wretched and lowly passions to point to the most sublime embodiment of Buddha. The scripture says, "Shariputra said to Vimalakirti, 'This seat is so high and wide that I cannot get up onto it.'" This is because the Two Vehicles of individual liberation totally empty passions, and want to see the embodiment of Buddha after that. How could they have figured that the eighty-four thousand passions themselves are the purple gold embodiment of reality, the mass of adornments, and the precious throne of all Buddhas?

This cannot be comprehended by those of inferior potential; so it was only appropriate that the disciple Shariputra could not get up onto the seat. Vimalakirti said, "Hey, Shariputra! Pay respects to the Wonderfully High Lamp King Buddha; then you can get a seat!"

And does the scripture not say that this Buddha presently exists? Where is the Lamp King Buddha right now? Don't make the mistake of gazing off toward the East past as many lands as sand grains in thirty-six Ganges Rivers! Is the Buddha not the independent wayfarer inherently complete in everyone, presently listening to the teaching? This is what Manjushri meant by saying that Buddha presently exists.

Once you have seen this, it is possible for a single atom to manifest countless thrones, and it is possible to contain countless thrones in a single atom. Whether you believe or not depends only on the degree of strength of your empowerment and the degree of depth of your perception. If it is remote, it is so remote that your spirit is desolate and your soul wiped out; if it is near, it is so near that subject and object both disappear.

The *Lotus of Truth* says, "All Buddhas take the emptiness of everything for their seat." The *Treatise on Wisdom* says, "Wherever a Buddha sits, be it in a chair or on the ground, it is always called a lion throne, as a lion walks alone among the four-legged beings, fearlessly subduing all." The *Book on Buddha Lands* says, "The lands of the Buddha are like space." This is the same thing as the seat of universal emptiness; how could it be like a worldly piece of furniture, fashioned and carved into an object of value?

The scripture says, "The enlightening being then transformed his body to be forty-two thousand leagues tall, and sat on the lion throne." A summary commentary says, "Earlier, it was explained that the Buddha is eighty-four thousand leagues tall; now, the enlightening being, in the state of cause, deferring effect, is only half as tall." This is also imperfect. The eighty-four thousand passions of all living beings are at once the true reality body of the Buddhas. Even enlightening beings, once they have comprehended this, rely on four kinds of committed practice and embody two forms of action, for themselves and for others; that seems to be the reason for speaking of "forty-two" thousand.

The narrow interpretation I have done here is not far-fetched. In ancient times, the Great Master of Sokei took the "hundred and eight lands" between here and the Western Pure Land to mean the ten evils and the eight perversions. Rinzai took "sitting for ten aeons on the site of enlightenment" to represent the ten transcendent ways. Another ancient worthy took "carrying oil for twenty-five miles" to refer to existence in the twenty-five mundane states of being. I am not imitating the sages, just amending abbreviated commentaries and incomplete texts.

47

It may be asked whether I mean we should wholly ignore phenomena and hold to noumenon. The answer is no. There is no noumenon outside of phenomena. You should know this. The Cardinal of Eshin Temple said, "Equality without distinctions is not in accord with Buddhism, because it is wrong equality. Distinction without equality is not in accord with Buddhism, because it is wrong distinction."

Why so? "I can only enjoy it myself; I cannot present it to you."

The Lesser Vehicles

In his essay "The Sands of Forty-two Ganges Rivers," Hakuin gives another symbolic interpretation of the number forty-two. Since this is not the same as his previous analysis, here Hakuin also explains how his reading differs according to context.

In this case, Hakuin takes forty-two to stand for the four truths and the twelve conditions, which are basic points of Buddhist teaching, frameworks of elementary Buddhist practices.

The four truths are the fact of suffering, the cause of suffering, the end of suffering, and the way to end suffering. The twelve conditions are these: ignorance conditions action, action conditions consciousness, consciousness conditions name and form, name and form condition sense media, sense media condition contact, contact conditions sensation, sensation conditions craving, craving conditions grasping, grasping conditions becoming, becoming conditions birth, birth conditions aging and death.

Followers of the so-called Two Vehicles of Hinayana or Lesser Vehicle Buddhism, who aim at individual illumination, focus on these phenomena and strive to transcend them through insight. Their goal is nirvana, perfect inner peace.

The Sands of Forty-two Ganges Rivers

In the *Pure Name Scripture*, the Book on the Buddha named Mass of Fragrance says, "In the zenith, past as many Buddha lands as grains

48

of sand in forty-two Ganges Rivers, there is a land called Many Fragrances." Generally, when scriptures speak of the grains of sand in the Ganges River, or in two Ganges Rivers, or in three Ganges Rivers, even up to thirty-six Ganges Rivers, forty-two Ganges Rivers, and so on, they are referring to unthinkable numbers, inconceivable calculations; but definition of numbers like thirty-six or forty-two usually has a symbolic basis.

When I had reached this point in my lectures, I wanted to find some proof, so I looked through a few commentaries; when I looked at the business about grains of sand in forty-two Ganges Rivers, I found that some commentators didn't deal with it at all, while some were dubious and uncertain.

Then someone produced a notebook stating that an explanation did exist, written by Great Master Yomei (Yung-ming) himself. The note said, "The twenty-fifth scroll of the *Source Mirror Record* says, 'To say that the Mass of Fragrance is as many worlds away from here as grains of sand in forty-two Ganges Rivers means passing through the teachings and methods of the forty-two stages of mind.'" Now, the mirror of Great Master Yomei's wisdom was high and clear, and the measure of his knowledge was immensely vast, beyond the powers of the likes of us even to conceive; and yet there remains some doubt.

I have heard that the Land of Common Abode is inhabited by both ordinary people and saints, the Land of Expediency with Remainder is inhabited by those of the Two Vehicles, the Land of Arrays of True Rewards is inhabited by enlightening beings, and the Land of Eternal Silent Light is inhabited only by Buddhas. Passing through forty-two stages, as the note said, refers to forty-two stages as defined in the *Flower Ornament Scripture*, through which forty-two grades of the Middle Way are realized. Is this not the attainment of complete Buddhahood, the Land of Eternal Silent Light inhabited only by Buddhas? Yet in the scripture it says, "At that time, the Buddha had just sat down to a meal with the enlightening beings. There were demigods there, all called Array of Fragrance." Clearly this is not the Land of Eternal Silent Light inhabited only by Buddhas!

All throughout, this scripture rebukes the bias and narrowness of

49

the Two Vehicles, and brings out the great potential of enlightening beings. Therefore, what the scripture refers to as passing as many lands as grains of sand in forty-two Ganges Rivers means passing beyond the Land of Expediency with Remainder inhabited by the Two Vehicles, which are based on the four truths and the twelve links of conditioning, pointing to the Land of Arrays of True Rewards inhabited by great enlightening beings.

What is the reasoning behind this? The scripture says, "In that land, even the names of followers and individual illuminates do not exist; there are only pure great enlightening beings, for whom the Buddha expounds the Teaching." From this perspective the sands of forty-two Ganges Rivers seem to stand for the four truths and the twelve conditions. Let the knowledgeable discern.

Absorption in Extinction

In his brief essay "The Seventh Consciousness Stabilization," Hakuin deals with a problematic technical term whose traditional interpretation seems to be unclear.

Hakuin's understanding is that this term, "the seventh consciousness stabilization," actually refers to the so-called absorption in extinction trance, in which all sense and perception are transcended by extinction. This trance was cultivated by ancient "Hindu" ascetics who mistook it for nirvana, and by certain followers of Buddhism who originally used it to prepare for nirvana but later also came to mistake it for nirvana itself.

The manner in which Hakuin integrates this practice into universalist Mahayana pan-Buddhism is metaphysically and inspirationally accurate, but yet it reveals a specific problem, a weakness within Hakuin's own practice, that also manifests particular problematic effects in the schools of his followers, who came to dominate later Rinzai Zen in Japan.

The Seventh Consciousness Stabilization

The seventh book of the *Pure Name Scripture*, on the Buddha Way, says, "The seventh consciousness stabilization is a seed." Kumarajiva comments, "In the first stage of meditation, after the Brahma King state and the Minor Brahma states at the beginning of the aeon, the rest is one consciousness stabilization." It seems to me that this comment of Kumarajiva's appears to be inaccurate; perhaps there was something he did not see through completely. Based on what scripture are the various Brahma states in the beginning of the aeon in the first meditation divided into seven consciousnesses? Subsequently the interpretation also says this should be seven compulsions, but that appears to have no clear basis. The meaning of seventh consciousness is imperfect, and the word *stabilization* is not sharply defined. Therefore I will give a summary presentation of my narrow view, as a gift of dharma, leaving it up to you whether you take it or leave it.

It seems to me that the "seventh consciousness stabilization" refers to the empty concentration practiced by outsiders, or the absorption in extinction practiced by those in the Two Vehicles of Hinayana Buddhism. When they want to attain these concentrations, they work toward the stillness of the depths of the storage consciousness, constantly fearing that they will run to the doings of the sensual and cognitive consciousnesses. However, although they avoid galloping to the sensual and cognitive consciousnesses, they have not yet attained the fruit of the Way, and cannot withdraw into the storage consciousness itself. They remain in the realm of the intellectual consciousness, the seventh consciousness, where they pass aeons. This is called the "seventh consciousness stabilization."

Question: Are not voidness and extinction both false concentrations? Later on in the scripture, they are referred to as a high plateau, or dry ground. How can they be referred to as seeds of Buddhahood?

Answer: When practitioners' minds suddenly open up clearly in concentration, the light of insight shines forth, splitting even an atomic particle to reveal the whole body of Vairochana Buddha. Then demons and Buddhas are one suchness, wrong and right are simultaneous. All beings, animate and inanimate, are all without exception elements of the seed of Buddhas.

As for the metaphor of the high plateau and dry ground, this scripture embodies nonduality to perform a critical function, driving the small toward the great. This is the only reason for such talk. In fact, all beings have Buddha-nature, so how could anything not be of the seed of Buddhas? Ha, ha!

The Solar Eclipse

Imagery and symbolism from ancient Indian mythology were naturally used by early Buddhists drawing instructional materials from the local environment. This does not imply a fixed belief structure on the part of Buddhists using this lore, but it does reflect belief structures of the people to whom the Buddha and the original Buddhists were addressing their talks. In technical terms, this docetic use of elements from the host culture is called *upaya-kaushalya* or "skill in means."

Such is the nature of repetitive traditionalism, however, that even followers of Buddhism would in time forget the provisional nature of their didactic constructs, taking the figurative literally. In his essay "The Titan Rahula Eclipsing the Sun," Hakuin responds to a question based on just such a misunderstanding. The specious nature of many "culture gap" arguments against Buddhism in non-Indian civilizations (including modern Western cultures) is clearly illustrated here, as Hakuin again demonstrates the method of reaching through and beyond superficial surface content to recover essential structures and thus inner meanings.

The Titan Rahula Eclipsing the Sun

Once when I was giving a series of lectures on the *Lotus of Truth* scripture in the 1740s, one day a monk came to my room, paid his respects, and said, "A commentary on the *Lotus of Truth* scripture says that 'Rahula' means obstructing; that is, obstructing the sun and moon. When the titan Rahula holds up his hand, he blocks the sun, and people think there is a solar eclipse; and when he blocks out the moon, they think there's a lunar eclipse. I have always been confused about this.

"Lately the Shintoists and Confucians get together and jeer at the Buddhists for ideas like this explanation of solar eclipses, denying their validity and abandoning them. Buddhists say that when the titans fought the king of gods, the celestial army was defeated in battle and fled, so the titan Demon King gained great power; he stood up in the ocean, grabbed the sun and moon, and made them go dark; so all solar and lunar eclipses are his doing.

"This explanation is very suspicious. Most solar eclipses occur near the end of the lunar month, while most lunar eclipses occur near the beginning of the lunar month. Let us reflect carefully; why would the celestial army take defeat three or four times a year? And why confine their defeats to the end and the beginning of the lunar month? If the celestials lose in battle every year, then the sun will invariably be eclipsed; if a lunar eclipse means an invariable loss in battle, when did this war begin, and when will it end? Might it go on for billions of aeons?

"And what about these calendrists—are they wizards or Buddhas with supernatural powers? Even military scientists cannot predict victory and defeat with certainty, and yet the calendrists see the state of affairs of celestial immortals 178,500 miles above like looking at a piece of fruit in their hands, and can accurately calculate the eclipses of the solar and lunar palaces in the hands of the titan. Determining the directions of risings and settings, from the west, east, or north, they print this up to circulate it. Calendrists say they can figure out the calendar accurately even decades ahead of time; they say none of the celestial bodies are beyond them, and that their science is so marvelous that their calculations cannot be mistaken even if fire might be made cool and water may be made hot. They say their art is incomparably superior to the nonsensical doctrines of the Buddhists.

"Now, I have been totally unable to respond to these challenges; what do you think of all this?"

My reply was that I had also doubted this doctrine for a long time. This doctrine is expounded in various scriptures, but the statement that people refer to the phenomena in question as solar and lunar eclipses is the statement of the questioner—I have never read this. The Great Teacher of Tendai went into the treasury of Vairochana fifteen times, memorized what he found, and expounded it; why couldn't he have a contemplative interpretation of this issue? What a pity not to have heard the lofty discourse of the great teacher! There must be such an explanation—could the record have been lost over time?

Buddha originally had three kinds of discourse: discourse on principle, metaphorical discourse, and explanation of causality. The doctrine in question here is a metaphorical discourse, in which illusory things of the world are used to illustrate true reality. You folks with the eyes of goats and sheep and the intelligence of foxes and badgers merely see the illusory things of the world and cannot understand the truth as it really is. Thus you arbitrarily slight the words of the enlightened. Once you've fallen into hell, there is no hope of getting out. What a pity!

For my recent lectures on the scripture, I used the *Terminology* commentary by the Master of Tendai, which says, " 'Rahula' means obstructing; this is a beast who obstructs the sun and moon. His body is eighty-four thousand leagues tall, his mouth is a thousand leagues wide." I finally realized that this is referring to basic ignorance as the titan Rahula.

What is the reason? The titan has quite a bit of supernatural power: when he wins in battle, he manifests a gigantic body so huge it makes the sky seem narrow and the ocean seem shallow; when he loses in battle, he manifests a tiny body, leading his eighty-four thousand followers into the holes in lotus threads to hide. Obviously the size of the titan's body is inconceivable in terms of tall or short; it is infinite, so why is it said to be eighty-four thousand leagues?

Here the king of gods stands for the mind monarch, the eighth consciousness, the storage consciousness. The titan Rahula stands for basic ignorance; eighty-four thousand leagues represent the eighty-four thousand passions in the cave of ignorance, while the thousand-league mouth stands for the ten evils. The sun and moon stand for the light of intelligence inherent in everyone, the primal uncreated sun of wisdom.

Buddha said, "Rahula does not swallow the sun and moon; Rahula's limbs quiver, running with sweat." If one practices single-mindedly, the ancient Buddha, long realized, finally appears; then the titan Rahula and his eighty-four thousand troops suddenly lose their whole bodies—they don't merely break out in a sweat!

What a pity that people cannot all bring forth the eternal Buddha inherent within them! Who knows how many are sitting on the site of enlightenment with their sun of wisdom eclipsed? This is called the perpetual solar eclipse of birth and death.

The Eight Consciousnesses

Ever since its origins in China, authentic Zen has always been intimately connected with classical Buddhist teachings and traditions. Many of the great Zen masters in China, Korea, and Japan alike were also masters of other Buddhist schools, scriptures, and sciences.

The Buddhist *vijnanavada*, or "doctrine of consciousness," also called *yogacara*, or "practice of unification," is one of the main veins of Mahayana Buddhism with which Zen is traditionally associated from its very foundation. Central to the psychological science of this element of Buddhism is the doctrine of the eight consciousnesses, a construct used to describe the totality and distinction of the main functions of mind.

In his essay "The Eight Princes," Hakuin takes an image from a scriptural story of eight royal princes to symbolize the eight consciousnesses. Then he proceeds to define and describe the eight consciousnesses, with remarkable skill in spite of the paucity of his formal learning, and as ever with energetic central reference to pragmatic and experiential realities underlying the terms and symbols he is using.

Finally, to conclude this essay Hakuin runs through a whole series of other scriptural images illustrating the vast range of function inherent in the eighth consciousness, which is the so-called storage consciousness constituting the ground of personal experience. Characteristically manifesting his emphasis on *kensho*, Hakuin relates this entire spectrum of imagery symbolizing mental function to the Zen practice of direct perception.

The Eight Princes

The introductory chapter of the *Lotus of Truth* scripture says, "The last Buddha, before leaving society, had eight royal children. The first was named Imbued with Intelligence." A commentary says, "The ancient Buddha had eight children, the present Buddha had one child. The one and the eight are conditional; they are just different representations. 'One' stands for the purity of the one Way; 'eight' stands for the eightfold right path."

When I read this, I thought to myself that this comment is not very precise. The Great Teacher of Tendai said that contemplations can be found in every passage of this scripture: since these eight princes are an important theme, how could there be no contemplative interpretation? The musings of sages of the past are not to be treated lightly, but I have a private opinion that I cannot suppress when it comes to lecturing, so I will set forth a wretched analysis to offer my colleagues. It is not for everyone; whether to take it or leave it is up to your own discriminating perception of things.

According to my analysis, the eight princes seem to represent the eight consciousnesses—the storage, intellectual, cognitive, and five sense consciousnesses. The father of the princes, whose name as a Buddha was Lamp Like the Sun and Moon, stands for the ninth consciousness, pure consciousness. This is called fundamental true cognition, or the universal mirroring cognition. Mine of Virtue, the enlightening being who received guidance for the future from the Lamp Buddha, represents temporal knowledge attained in the aftermath of awakening.

If practitioners progress singlemindedly without flagging or backsliding, thinking will disappear, emotional thoughts will vanish, and the mind source will be profoundly still, unmoving, unstirring, like space itself, thoroughly clear, absolutely spotless. This is called the eighth domain, the storage consciousness; this is the vanguard and the rearguard, the root of birth and death, that which contains all elements, good and bad. That which flows very subtly therein, inconspicuously recollecting and holding memories, is called the seventh consciousness, the communicating, transmitting, intellectual consciousness. Herein there is something that appears and disappears in the media of the five senses, grasping and rejecting myriad objects, swift as the wind, fast as lightning, always clamorous, ever in an uproar; this is called the sixth consciousness, the cognitive consciousness.

The eyes can see colors and forms, but do not distinguish between beautiful and ugly. The nose can smell scent, but does not know the fragrant from the foul. The ears can hear sounds, but do not make a distinction between the melodious and the harsh. The body can feel texture, but does not discriminate between the soft and the slippery. These are called the primary five consciousnesses; these five and the eighth consciousness have no discrimination, while the sixth and seventh consciousnesses have cognitive knowledge.

Although the primary five have no cognitive knowledge, each has a specific capacity, so they are named Imbued with Intelligence. They have no false ideas whatsoever, so they are called Good Intelligence.

The sixth, or cognitive, consciousness contains the pivots of qualification and quantification, so it is named Infinite Intelligence. Once practitioners are inspired, by skillful application of expedient techniques they will ultimately reach the Treasure Trove of complete enlightenment; this is the same thing, so it is called Precious Intelligence.

The seventh, or intellectual, consciousness is that which transmits information, understands sayings, and looks to deeds of the past, always helping completion of work on the Way; so it is called Enhancing Intelligence. With accurate beliefs and comprehensive understanding, it removes subtle delusions; therefore it is called Doubt-Removing Intelligence.

As for the eighth, or storage, consciousness, on examination it proves to be wide open, immaterial and unmoving, utterly formless; but the instant it is stimulated it exercises its subtle functions in the media of the six senses, just as an empty valley transmits echoes. Thus it is called Echoing Intellect. The formless empty valley, as described above, contains all things—compounded phenomena, uncompounded phenomena, living beings, ten realms, ten suchnesses, a hundred realms, a thousand suchnesses; one transformation, and there is only the reality of one vehicle to complete enlightenment. So it is called True Intelligence.

Question: Since the seventh and eighth consciousnesses do have distinctions, why do they all come with the name Intelligence?

Answer: Though the primary five and the seventh and eighth do seem to be distinct, the sneaky intellect haunts them, making them its own playground, so it always seems that there is intellect in each and every sense medium; so they all get the name Intelligence. Basically they are the unborn eight children of the house of unchanging suchness, born according to conditions through the relations of illusory object parents.

Some speak of the eighth consciousness as the mind king. The *Pure Name Scripture* calls this the deep dark pit of ignorance in the world of immobility; this is what whirls around in front of living beings, transforming the crystal mirror of actions into the iron tablet of the king of hell. If practitioners cultivate it single-mindedly and succeed in bringing it out, then it turns out to be the universal mirroring cognition, while the intellect is then the cognition of equality. The sixth, cognitive, consciousness becomes precise observing cognition, and the five primary consciousnesses become practical cognition.

All of these are subtle functions inherent in the universal mirror. The billion-world universe, the Buddha-fields numerous as grains of sand in the Ganges River, heavens and hells, ghost lands and devil palaces, are all reflections appearing in the shine of the universal mirror.

Since it reflects everything, it is called the Buddha Lamp Bright as Sun and Moon. The *Pure Name Scripture* calls it the Buddha Wonderfully High Lamp.

All the Buddhas of all times and places are thus. It is quite fitting for two trillion Buddhas to have the same epithet. Not only two trillion—Buddhas as numerous as grains of sand in a hundred thousand trillion Ganges Rivers are thus!

Question: If so, then is it not an incalculable number? Why only speak of two trillion?

Answer: Good question! There is duality in all things and all beings. For example, when the two modes of energy divide, there are heaven and earth, there are yin and yang; thence the four forms, eight trigrams, and sixty-four hexagrams occur in an orderly process. Ruler and subject, father and son, husband and wife, old and young, high and low, intelligent and stupid, skillful and inept, moving and still, painful and pleasant, self and other, that and this, right and wrong, beautiful and ugly, hate and love, familiar and strange, light and dark, form and void, being and nonbeing, gain and loss, long and short, activity and rest, poor and rich, rising and falling, giving and taking. As echo to sound, as shadow to form, as soon as a single atom comes into being, duality inevitably occurs.

This duality pervades all phenomena, without exception. That is why scriptures often speak of places as twenty leagues square, and say that true teaching will last for twenty medium aeons, and that imitation teaching will also last twenty medium aeons. Obviously the number two is universal.

So it is truly ridiculous the way medieval canonical scholars erased the word *trillion* lest the number be too great. I have heard there were texts that had the word *trillion*, and Prince Shotoku of Japan, lamenting that the versions that came to Japan lacked this word, went to a temple on a sacred mountain in China to find one. I used to think that since there were sixty-nine thousand other characters to get caught up in, why did Prince Shotoku care and fuss so much about the one word *trillion?* Now I see it is very valuable!

The scripture also says, "And they all have the same surname, Bharadvaja." The Hsu commentary cites a work in which this name is translated as Double Banner. When I read this, the rhinoceros of doubt suddenly opened its eyes. Why? Because the word *banner* is quite contrary to the intent of the scripture. It should be *pupil*. There must have been a copyist's error, for the Chinese characters are similar.

Now I looked through dozens of copies of the scripture brought to the lectures by members of the audience, but none of them had the word *pupil*. I thought to myself that even if others write "Banner," I will change it to "Pupil" and analyze it that way. Why? Because the pupil of the eye is quintessential to the whole body; and the double pupil is a sign of a sage! Bharadvaja, or Double Pupils, must represent the two kinds of knowledge of Buddhas, temporal and absolute. Why? Knowledge is the eye of living beings, and the two kinds of knowledge are the lifeline of the Buddhas. Who could reject this explanation?

But it also occurred to me that the Banner name may have been gotten as a result of having made offerings of banners and canopies to Buddhas in the past. If that is so, I make a dunce of myself. Too bad there are no good translators around. Here the rhinoceros of doubt suddenly nodded.

Then a monk came with a notebook, saying it was Master Koyo Toko's special study, written in crimson. This notebook cited a reference to the book on the three Kashyapa brothers in the scripture *Compendium of Past Deeds*, which says, "Bharadvaja means Double Pupils. The traditional version of the Hsu commentary is mistaken." When I saw this, I felt as though I had found a jade lamp on a road at night. The rhinoceros of doubt now relaxed again.

Scripture also says, "Then the Buddha Lamp Like the Sun and Moon arose from absorption, and sat unstirring for sixty minor aeons expounding the Great Vehicle scripture called the Lotus of Truth, teachings for enlightening beings, kept in mind by all Buddhas, at the instance of the enlightening being Sublime Light. At that time, the audience also sat in one place for sixty minor aeons, unmoving in body and mind, listening to what the Buddha said, thinking the time passing to be as that required to eat a meal. No one in the audience flagged, either physically or mentally."

This is the secret of the scripture, but it is a critical point that is hard to believe in, hard to understand, hard to penetrate, and hard to enter into. Never mind people like the practitioners of the deer park of Buddha's time; even people of mature potential for the special teaching or the complete teaching may doubt or slight this. Why? Because people may be young or old, strong or weak, long-lived or short-lived, intelligent or stupid, but no one can sit like a rock unflagging for sixty minor aeons without eating or sleeping. Is it not fitting that Confucians and Shintoists point this out as an example of Buddhist nonsense?

While it is inappropriate to mix up a profound principle such as this with arbitrary interpretations, I will attempt an explanation.

The sixty minor aeons represent the six fields of sense; nothing in the world is beyond the six sense fields. When the Lamp Buddha expounded the Lotus of Truth, at the same time rivers, birds, trees, and forests expounded it and listened to it simultaneously; a billion aeons were equal to a fingersnap, so there could be no flagging at all.

What is right before you at this moment?

Who would have known? The Diamond Scripture's statement that all kinds of living beings are initiated by Buddha into nirvana without remainder is the same pattern as the absorption in the Lotus of Truth entered by people suited for the complete teaching. Do not say that transcendent wisdom is like curd, the culmination of a gradual process, whereas the Lotus of Truth is like ghee, characterized by completeness and balance. Is that not a contradiction?

Why? Space gnashes its teeth at midnight.

Experiential Time

In his essay "Fifty Minor Aeons in the Book on Emergence from Earth," Hakuin deals with an image from the beloved *Saddhar-mapundarika-sutra*, or *Lotus of Truth Scripture*, one of the very greatest of the universalist Buddhist texts. The *Lotus of Truth* reveals the teaching of *Ekayana* or One Vehicle Buddhism, which is at once the original ground and the ultimate expression of *Mahayana* or Great Vehicle Buddhism.

The basic principles of Ekayana Buddhism are that there is actually only one true objective reality, that all beings have the capacity for awareness of this reality in accord with their individual capacities, and that the overall teaching of Buddhism is therefore one unity, which is nevertheless received and absorbed in a variety of ways depending on the individual faculties of the hearers.

True to his central emphasis on kensho, Hakuin takes the universal Buddha-nature of the One Vehicle to mean the so-called One Mind, the basic ground of mind. With this realization, the fifty minor aeons are seen by Hakuin to symbolize the elements of all the possible states of sensation, perception, and existence within the totality of immediate experience.

Fifty Minor Aeons in the Book on Emergence from Earth

The fifth book of the *Lotus of Truth* scripture says, "These great enlightening beings emerged from the earth and lauded the Buddha with the praises of enlightening beings. Thus passed fifty minor aeons, during which Shakyamuni Buddha sat silently, and the people of the four groups also remained silent."

Some people say, "I have heard that the Buddha was one who did not lie, who did not speak at variance with truth. Even the gods salute the statements of Buddha's universal, perennial speech. This is not even conceivable to people like us." Nevertheless, there is something to be wondered at here, and I beg leave to attempt to discuss it.

The scripture says that the enlightening beings sang Buddha's praises for fifty minor aeons. Even one aeon is an immensely long time, to say nothing of fifty minor aeons. When the scripture says the Buddha was lauded for fifty minor aeons, to what Buddha does this refer? If it refers to our root teacher, the historical Buddha, the *Lotus of Truth* and *Ultimate Nirvana* scriptures were both expounded over a period of eight years; the Buddha himself was eighty years old when he passed away, and his disciple Ananda also died at the age of eighty. The rest of the eighty thousand Buddhist saints all died before living a full hundred years. So how could a Buddha who lived for eighty years be eulogized for fifty minor aeons? How very strange!

A Tendai commentary says, "It is like when people are in pain, a short time seems like a long time; when people are having fun, a long time seems like a short time. This is simply a representation of respect for the teaching." The *Notes on Phraseology* says, "Causing fifty minor aeons to seem like half a day illustrates the Buddha's inconceivable capacity to expand and contract time, revealing the Buddha's power of independence."

These interpretations are quite inaccurate; they can be called arbitrary explanations. Leaving aside for the moment the Buddha's power to expand and contract time independently, where do the fifty minor aeons fit in the eight-year period? The populations of cities where Buddha taught, like Benares and Vaisali, furthermore, would have passed away without a trace in fifty aeons.

People will say that time may be expanded as much as Buddha may, but there is no such thing as fifty minor aeons! Consider the fact that Buddha was a free man, but since there was so much benefit to people in seeing him manifest spiritual powers, eventually he couldn't but wind up displaying miraculous capacities. Now what about here where he expands half a day to fifty minor aeons—which of the eighty thousand people there gained great benefit? Were there no benefit, it would just be a bit of childish sport. It would be enough to speak of eulogizing Buddha for half a day—why go to the trouble of making it into fifty minor aeons?

People may experience a lifetime of ups and downs in the brief space of a dream; certainly it is within the capacity of a Buddha with Ten Powers to expand a half day into fifty aeons, but what is the basis for contracting fifty aeons into half a day? What is the proof?

Suppose someone is assailed by all sorts of pains and miseries; he considers half a day on this earth to be fifty minor aeons in hell. When the universal compassion of Buddha rescues him, it can be said to have contracted fifty minor aeons to half a day. You can also call it a Buddha's power to expand and contract time independently.

Even though they are rootless, if we say fifty minor aeons are contracted into half a day, some people will surely say this is typical Buddhist nonsense. In recent times, it often happens that Confucians or Shintoists hear tell of talk like this, and slight Buddhism because they cannot fathom its mysterious subtlety, calling it meaningless, useless, and unworthy of belief. This is actually fitting; even we Buddhists, who believe and apply every word of the teachings, cannot be free of doubt, so how can others, ignorant incorrigibles whose crimes of repudiating truth will land them in hell! Now if someone of high intelligence were to oppose Buddhism lucidly enough to cause it serious harm, that would really be frightening!

I too have a little interpretation, which I'd like to bring up. The scripture clearly says that Shakyamuni Buddha sat silently, and so did the other members of the four groups. This is the eye of the chapter. Tell me, does this silent sitting refer to the present? Is it the Other Side, transcendent? Is it lifeless sitting in oblivious silence? Is it gazing on the ocean of knowledge?

As for Spiritual Mountain, let us leave this aside for the moment. What about the old man and the four groups now sitting in this enlightenment site—are they stirring or still? Are they ordinary ignoramuses, or are they wise sages?

When you can see clearly, I'll admit that you have personally penetrated the fifty minor aeons. As soon as you have understood fifty minor aeons, when you see "sitting silently," then at that precise time heaven and hell are silent, Buddha-fields and demon-realms are also silent—what is strange about fifty minor aeons? Otherwise, have you even dreamed of seeing the *Lotus of Truth*, scripture of the complete doctrine of the Great Vehicle?

The scripture also says that this time during which Buddha was eulogized lasted fifty minor aeons. What does this mean? "This time" is the impenetrable mystery of the scripture: fifty minor aeons *are* "this time," and "this time" *is* itself fifty minor aeons. Here the fields of the five senses, the five clusters, the five major constituents, and the five elements join to make fifty minor aeons; seen with the true eye, all are not beyond the instant of the moment of awareness of the immediate present.

Question: If so, then a thousand lifetimes, myriad aeons, even trillions of aeons, are not at all beyond the instant of the immediate present—why particularly choose to indicate fifty minor aeons? You say all phenomena are not beyond the fields of the five senses—form, sound, and so on—and all conscious beings are not beyond the five clusters of matter, sensation, and so on. Even if it only says fifty minor aeons, ultimately it is a numberless number, a measureless measure; it is the instant where language reaches an impasse, where mental construction has no object, where all sages and saints lay down their bodies and give up their lives. At this the eulogies of Buddha stop, the vow to disseminate the scripture is complete, and both animate and inanimate beings attain enlightenment and become Buddhas at the same time. This is the marrow of the scripture, and the basis of its saying that "there is only One Vehicle, not two, and not three." Please give me a testimony.

Answer: You're right, but unfortunately you still lack the breakthrough. Your statement is an ordinary intellectual explanation playing with a mud ball.

This principle is the hard-to-penetrate secret of the scripture, the hard-to-believe mystery, a manifest expression of the Buddha's great compassionate skill in means. Buddhas and Zen illuminates commonly use this secret to guide those of the very highest potential; mediocre and lesser people cannot even dream of seeing it. This is why the Buddha said, "My disciples who have attained sainthood cannot understand this principle; only great enlightening beings can understand it." How true!

This principle is an essential route of dissemination of the scripture in latter days, a golden broth to preserve the teaching in a polluted era. If my students comprehend this principle, they will abruptly transcend the gradual process of four stages of realization and three stages of wisdom, to arrive immediately at the treasure trove of the great enlightening beings.

Now then, the most advanced people involved in study of the mysterious will know the point at a glance. If you turn to your dead notebooks and talk about what this, that, and the other commentary has to say, you will never pass through. Why? Because you are actually repudiating the scripture, and this is the punishment you get for it.

If you want to understand this principle truly and correctly, first you must actually see the true countenance of the lotus of truth. If you want to see the true countenance of the lotus of truth, you must see your own true nature. Once you have seen your own true nature, you will immediately comprehend the principle in question and directly perceive the true countenance of the lotus of truth.

This is why the *Nirvana Scripture* says that enlightening beings perceive Buddha-nature visually, and it also says that those who attain to realization of suchness see Buddha-nature with their eyes. The founder of Zen also said, "If people want to fulfill the Way of Buddhas, first they should see essential nature."

Why? If children aren't used to seeing chariots and horses, they'll scurry off and hide in the reeds.

The Five Ranks

The classical masters of the golden age of Zen in China—the eighth through the tenth centuries—devised a considerable range of symbolic systems to encapsulate the essentials of their teachings, practices, and experiences. One such device is the famous Five Ranks of Absolute and Relative, which was developed by the Chinese masters Tung-shan (Japanese, Tozan) and Ts'ao-shan (Sozan) in the ninth century.

The roots of the origin of the Five Ranks are to be found in the contemplative metaphysics of the Flower Ornament school of Chinese Buddhism, with which all the classical Zen masters were familiar. The Five Ranks are also represented symbolically in the *Lotus of Truth* scripture, which was commonly read and recited by Chinese Zen Buddhists as well as followers of other schools. In Chinese Zen literary tradition, the core of the Five Ranks is found in a work called *Focusing the Precious Mirror*, which was transmitted by Tung-shan (Tozan) from his forbears to his successor Ts'ao-shan (Sozan). The former master defined the Five Ranks and elucidated them in verse; the latter master and his heir Ts'ao-shan II expressed them in prose and used them to make structural analyses of Zen Kung-an (Japanese, koan), stories for awakening and enlightening the mind.

In Hakuin's time (nearly one thousand years after the passing of the classical masters), the policies of the feudal Japanese government fostered formalism, no matter how arid, in all domains of life, including religion. Buddhist clerics, even in Zen, were encouraged to devote themselves to ceremony and scholastic study, with the result that an enormous quantity of vapid and buddhistically sterile ritual, liturgy, and scholarship was produced in those days.

The unsurpassed metaphysical and sapiential subtleties of the Five Ranks were evidently lost on generations of Japanese Zen Buddhist scholars, and a particularly large volume of nonsense was written on this subject, along with a few truly accurate and insightful works. Hakuin took a special interest in the Five Ranks, perhaps on account of his own teacher's emphasis on this system, and probably also because of his own frustration in trying to find authentic masters in the Soto school of Zen, through which the Five Ranks were largely transmitted until that time.

Hakuin's own approach to the Five Ranks is purely pragmatic. He does not enter into philosophical or literary comment but confines himself to the Five Ranks as successive aspects of Zen practice and experience. Hakuin's descriptions of these stages, furthermore, are not abstract psychology but vivid accounts of the inner states engendered along the path of Zen. In the course of this discussion, Hakuin explains the need for progressive practice and gradual refinement, dismissing oversimplified and subjectively biased approaches to Zen as ineffective and unworthy.

Secrets of the Five Ranks of Soto Zen

Focusing the Precious Mirror says, "In the six lines of the double *Fire* hexagram, relative and absolute interchange. Piled up, they make three; when the transformation is complete, they make five."

The authorship of *Focusing the Precious Mirror* is unknown. It was transmitted secretly from master to master—from Sekito to Yakuzan to Ungan—without being leaked out to easy access. When it was transmitted to Master Tozan, he was the first to write about the grades of the five ranks, tagging a verse to each rank in order to bring out the overall pattern of the Buddha Way. This could be called a precious lamp on a dark road, a boat or a raft over the harbor of confusion.

How sad is the aridity of contemporary Zen schools! They laud unintelligent ignorance as transcendental direct-pointing Zen. Considering unsurpassed spiritual treasures like *Focusing the Precious Mirror* and the Five Ranks to be worn-out utensils of an antiquated house, they pay no attention to them. They are like blind people throwing away their canes, saying they are useless, then getting them-

68

selves stuck in the mud of the view of elementary realization, never able to get out all their lives.

In particular, they do not know that the Five Ranks are a ship across the poison sea of the absolute state, a precious discus spinning through the prison of the two voids. Since they do not know the essential road of progressive cultivation, and are unfamiliar with these secrets, they sink into the stagnant water of followers and individual illuminates, stumble into the dark pit of scorched sprouts and spoiled seeds, eventually reaching the point where even Buddha himself could hardly save them.

What I received from Shoju Rojin forty years ago, I now offer as a donation of teaching to genuine students of the mystery who have experienced the great death. This should be handed on privately, because it was not set up for people of middling and lesser potential. Make sure not to take it too lightly!

Ah, the ocean of the teaching is immensely vast, with countless doctrines and methods. Among them are esoteric transmissions and secrets passed on by word of mouth, but I have never seen anything corrupted like the Five Ranks. Tedious commentaries on the double *Fire* hexagram and hair-splitting discourses on "piling" and "transformation" add branches to branches, tie vines to vines, ultimately ignorant of the principle for which the Five Ranks were set up. This makes students all the more confused, so that it seems even the most intelligent have a hard time discerning.

Did our ancestors indeed produce nonsense, burdening their descendants for no reason? I wondered about this for a long time, until I studied with Shoju, whereupon the rhinoceros of my former doubt dropped dead. If learners practice progressively on this basis, it will be very beneficial. Do not doubt it on the grounds that it is not a word-of-mouth transmission from a teacher in the Soto tradition. You should know that Shoju made a special study of Tozan's verses before he made his analysis. Do not slight it on the grounds that it is not a word-of-mouth transmission from a teacher in the Soto tradition!

There are many complicated explanations of the meanings of interchange, piling up, and transformation. Among them, people talk about the analyses of two Ming dynasty Chinese writers. Taking the second, third, and fourth lines from the six lines of the double *Fire* hexagram yields the *Wind* trigram, representing the relative within the absolute. Taking the third, fourth, and fifth lines yields the *Lake* trigram, representing the absolute within the relative. Then you see the hexagram *Great Surpassing,* with the lake trigram on top of the *Wind* trigram. Taking the second, third, and fourth lines from *Great Surpassing* yields the *Heaven* trigram, representing coming from the absolute. This is their interpretation of "piled up they make three." This seems fine, but when it comes to "when the transformation is complete, they make five," it is not so fine at all.

Eventually, when Shoju transmitted the teaching of the Five Ranks to me, only then did I have a sense of completeness. But even though I was satisfied, I still lamented that teachers had not completely analyzed the meaning of the interchange of relative and absolute, as if they have thrown away the word *interchange* and paid no attention to it. At this point the rhinoceros of doubt rose its head again.

In the summer of 1748, while in a state of concentration, I suddenly discovered the secret profundity of the interchange of relative and absolute, as clearly as if I were looking at the palm of my hand. The rhinoceros of doubt fell dead. I was so happy that I wanted to pass it on, but I was embarrassed to foul the mouths of seekers with some stinking pap I forced out.

If you want to find the profound source, you must search through personal experience. I have labored these thirty years—don't think it's easy! Unless you reach "destruction of the home," do not think your attainment sufficient; vow to penetrate all the way through seven, eight, even nine thickets of brambles. And when you have passed through the thickets of brambles, don't consider that enough either; vow to find out the secret of the Five Ranks.

For the last eight or nine years, I have wanted to encourage my colleagues to investigate this great matter, but time and again they have regarded it as the teaching of another sect, and have paid no attention to it. Unfortunately, there have only been a few exceptions to this. What about the vow to study the infinite teachings? Is this the universal order of the Buddha Way? Is this the essential road of Zen study?

Old Man Shoju said the master teachers first set up the Five Ranks as a compassionate expedient to get students to experience the four cognitions. This is quite different from doctrinal discourse.

The four cognitions are the universal mirrorlike cognition, cognition of equality, observing cognition, and practical cognition. Even if you have diligently cultivated discipline, concentration, and knowledge for many aeons, as long as you have not experienced the four cognitions you cannot be called true Buddhists.

When followers of the Way seek truly and correctly, so as to break through the dark cave of the storehouse of the eighth consciousness, the precious light of the universal mirror cognition immediately shines forth. But strangely enough, the light of the universal mirror is pitch black! This is called the rank of the relative absolute.

Here the universal mirror cognition is partially experienced; then you go on to enter the rank of the absolute relative. When you have cultivated the focusing of the precious mirror for a long time, if you actually succeed in realizing part of the cognition of equality for the first time you will enter the state of the realm of reality in which noumenon and phenomena are not separated.

This is still not enough for a practitioner; enter intimately into "coming from within the absolute," and by means of "arriving in both," you completely realize the four cognitions, including observing cognition and practical cognition. Ultimately you reach the rank of "attainment in both," whereupon "in the final analysis you return to sit in the ashes." What does this mean? Pure gold that has been refined ten thousand times does not become ore again.

The only thing to fear is considering a little attainment to be enough. The valuable thing about the Five Ranks, of relative and absolute, and of achievement and attainment, is that you thereby not only realize the four cognitions but also complete the three bodies in your being. Have you not read the *Adornment of the Universalist*

Scriptures where it says, "Transform the eight consciousnesses into the four cognitions; combine the four cognitions, and you have the three bodies." Therefore the great master of Sokei composed a verse saying,

> Your own nature
> contains the three bodies;
> when you discern them,
> they constitute the four cognitions.

He also said, "The pure reality body is your essential nature, the fulfilled reward body is your knowledge, and the infinitely multiplied emanation body is your activity."

Verses on the Five Ranks
by MASTER TOZAN RYOKAI

1
The Relative Absolute

> In the third watch,
> beginning of the night,
> before the moon is bright,
> do not wonder
> at meeting without recognition;
> still held hidden in the heart
> is the beauty of former days.

The rank of the relative absolute refers to the absolute state, where you experience the great death, explode, see the Way, and penetrate the noumenon. When genuine practitioners have built up accomplishment at inner seeking and are filled with the power of hidden cultivation, if they suddenly break through, then space itself vanishes and iron mountains shatter. Above, there is not a single tile to cover your head; below, there is not an inch of earth to stand upon. There is neither affliction nor enlightenment, no samsara or nirvana. It is

72

totally empty and still, with no sound, no scent, like a bottomless clear pool, like trackless space.

It often happens that people take this rank to be the end of the whole matter; considering it attainment of Buddhahood, they cling to it obsessively, never letting go. This is called Zen in stagnant water, where one becomes a ghost haunting a corpse in a coffin. Even if you spend thirty or forty years addicted to this state, you cannot get out of the cave of the minor attainment of individual awakening and self-understanding.

This is why it is said that if potential does not leave its state, it falls into an ocean of poison. This is what Buddha called the great fool who grasps realization in the absolute state. Even if you have clarified true cognition of equality, you cannot activate subtle observing cognition seeing all things without impediment. Therefore, although inside and out may be perfectly clear as long as you are hidden away in an unfrequented place where there is absolute quiet and nothing to do, yet you are powerless as soon as perception touches upon different worldly situations, with all their clamor and emotion, and you are beset by a plethora of miseries. It was in order to cure this serious illness that the rank of the absolute relative was defined.

The Absolute Relative
A woman who's overslept
encounters an ancient mirror;
clearly she sees her face—
there is no other reality.
Nevertheless, she still mistakes
her reflection for her head.

If practitioners become fixated on the rank of the relative absolute, their cognition is always affected by attraction and aversion and their point of view is biased. This is why enlightening beings of higher faculties always sit and recline in the midst of the variety of different situations in action; you see everything before your eyes as your own original true clean face, just as if you were looking at your face in a mirror.

Seeing everything in this way, over months and years all things become your own precious mirror, and you are their precious mirror. Dogen said, "Experiencing myriad things with the burden of the self is delusion; experiencing oneself in the manifestation of myriad things is enlightenment." That is what this means.

At this point, you are mentally and physically liberated, mind and body free and at ease. Like two mirrors reflecting each other without any image between them, mind and objects are one suchness, things and self are not separate. "A white horse goes into white flowers." "Snow piles up in a silver bowl." This is called focusing the precious mirror.

This is what the *Nirvana Scripture* refers to as those who realize suchness seeing Buddha-nature with their eyes. When you go into this focus, the "great white ox" will not go away even though pushed; cognition of equality appears right before you. This is what is meant by the saying that there is only one vehicle, the middle way, the manifestation of reality, the ultimate truth.

If learners who have reached this state consider it enough, then as enlightening beings they still fall at the peak into a deep pit. Why? They do not know the conduct of enlightening beings, and do not understand the conditions for a Buddha land. It was in order to remedy this problem that the masters went on to define the rank of coming from within the absolute.

Coming from Within the Absolute
Within nothingness is a road
out of the dust;
just be able to avoid violating
the present taboo name
and you will still surpass
the eloquence of yore
that silenced every tongue.

In this rank, enlightening beings of the higher vehicle do not dwell in the state of result they have realized; from the ocean of effortlessness, they radiate unconditional great compassion. Riding on the four universal pure vows, turning the wheel of teaching, seeking enlightenment above while edifying people below.

This is what is called coming back within going away, going away within coming back. It is also imperative to know there is a time when "light and dark are double pairs." Therefore the rank of arriving in both is also defined.

Arriving in Both
When two blades cross,
no need to flee;
an expert is like
a lotus in fire—
clearly there is a spirit
spontaneously soaring.

In this rank, powerful enlightening beings spin the wheel of the principle of nonduality of light and dark. In the midst of the red dust, ashes on the head and mud on the face, they act freely in the company of sound and form; like a lotus blossom whose color and fragrance become fresher and clearer in fire, they go into the marketplace extending their hands, acting for others.

This is what is called being on the road without leaving home, leaving home without being on the road. Is this an ordinary person? Is this a sage? Demons and outsiders cannot discern such a person; even Buddhas and Zen masters can do nothing.

If you excitedly try to aim for this, it is like rabbit horns and turtle hair gone to another mountain. Even this cannot be considered the place to sit in peace. That is why it is said that "clearly there is a spirit spontaneously soaring." What about the ultimate? You must know there is another rank, attainment in both.

Attainment in Both
If you are not trapped
in being or nonbeing,

75

who can dare to join you?
Everyone wants to leave
the ordinary current,
but in the final analysis
you come back
and sit in the ashes.

If learners want to pass through Tozan's rank of attainment in both,
you should first study the following verse:

That idle old awl Cloud of Virtue—
how many times has he come down
from the peak of wonder!
He helps other foolish sages
hauling snow to fill a well.

The Four Cognitions

The traditional Zen formula "seeing essence, realize enlightenment," originally intended to illustrate the ineffectiveness of formal knowledge and practice without inner perception of reality,
left Zen followers of later times with an overly simplified view of
what they were seeking. Because of Hakuin's tremendous emphasis on kensho, followers of his school also fell into this trap. In his
essay "The Four Cognitions," Hakuin counters such reductionist
tendencies by defining a succession of stages of realization in
which a more complete spectrum of human capacities gradually
unfolds.

The essay begins with the question of the relationship between sudden realization and gradual practice, between potential
and actualization. Here Hakuin represents fulfillment by means
of the classical Buddhist constructs of three bodies and four cognitions proper to Buddhahood.

The three bodies are the body of reality, which corresponds to essence, the body of perfect enjoyment, which corresponds to insight, and the body of emanation, which corresponds to activity. These three "bodies" of Buddhahood are associated with, or one might say imbued with, four kinds of cognition. The first of these four is called the universal mirroring cognition, which perceives things as they are without conceptual glosses, as if the mind were a mirror, impartially reflecting whatever comes before it. Second is cognition of equality, insight into the universal essence of things. Third is subtle observing cognition, which handles differentiation, in contrast to the nondiscursive and unitive nature of the first two cognitions. The fourth cognition, practical cognition, refers to action in harmony with the insight and knowledge realized through the other three forms of cognition. Altogether, these four constitute the total integrity of the enlightened mind.

As usual, Hakuin is sparing with abstract metaphysical technicalities, preferring to focus on praxis. In this essay, he shows how to pursue the Zen exercise of "turning the light around" through successive stages of refinement.

The Four Cognitions

Some ask, "Are the three bodies and four cognitions inherent, or are they in the sphere of knowledge attained after awakening? Are they realized all at once, or are they cultivated gradually?"

The answer is that even though these are fundamentally complete in everyone, they cannot be realized unless they are brought to light. When you have accumulated effort in study and investigation and the Buddha-nature suddenly appears, all at once you realize the essence of inner reality; all is attained in one attainment.

But even though you reach the stage of awakening without passing through steps and stages, if you do not cultivate practice gradually it will be impossible to fulfill omniscience, independent knowledge, and ultimate great enlightenment.

What is the meaning of realization all at once? When the discriminatory mentality is suddenly shattered and the essence of enlightenment suddenly appears, the filling of the universe with its boundless light is called the universal mirror cognition, the pure body of reality. This is the transmuted storage consciousness.

Realizing all things in the six fields of sense—seeing, hearing, discernment, and knowledge—are your own enlightened nature is called cognition of equality, the fulfilled body of perfect enjoyment.

Discerning the principles of things by the light of true knowledge is called subtle observing cognition. This is the body of perfect enjoyment, and also includes the emanation body.

Activity, stillness, even coughing and spitting and swinging the arms as you walk, all doings in harmony with the nature of reality are called practical cognition. This is called the sphere of freedom of the emanation body.

Even so, nevertheless your perception of the Way is not yet perfectly clear, and your power of shining insight is not yet fully mature. If you do not cultivate yourself, therefore, you will be like a merchant who keeps his capital and does not engage in trade. He does not prosper, and even goes bankrupt spending to keep up appearances.

Gradual cultivation is like a merchant devoting himself to trade, spending a hundred pieces of gold to make a thousand in profit. Eventually he accumulates boundless wealth and becomes free to do what he wishes with his bounty.

Although there is no difference in the nature of gold, it is impossible to get rich without doing business like this. Similarly, even if your perception of reality is genuine, you cannot overthrow the barriers of habitual actions as long as your power of shining insight is weak. Unless your knowledge of differentiation is clear, you cannot help people according to their potentials. Therefore you have to know the essential road of gradual cultivation.

What is the universal mirror cognition? When you want to comprehend this great matter, first you must develop great will and great faith; determined to see into your inherent Buddha-nature, you should constantly ask yourself who is hosting your seeing and hearing.

No matter what you are doing, whether you are walking, standing still, sitting down, or lying down, whether you are active or silent, whether you are in pleasant circumstances or unpleasant situations, plunge your spirit into this question: what is it that sees everything here and now? What is it that hears?

Questioning like this, pondering like this, wondering what it is, when you keep on wondering continuously, driven by courage and conscience, your effort will naturally become unified and solid, turning into a single mass of wonder pervading the universe. Your spirit is suffocated, your mind in distress, like a bird in a cage, like a rat that's crawled into a bamboo tube and cannot turn around.

At that time, if you keep on going without retreating, it will be like entering a crystal world: the whole mass, inside and outside, floors and ceilings, houses and buildings, fields and mountains, grasses and trees, people and animals, utensils and goods, are all as it were like illusions, like dreams, like shadows, like mist.

When you open your eyes with clear presence of mind and see with certainty, there appears an inconceivable realm that seems to exist yet also seems nonexistent in a way. This is called the time when the nature of consciousness becomes manifest. If you think this is wonderful and extraordinary, and you gladly become infatuated and attached to this experience, after all you will fall into the nests of the two vehicles of individual deliverance, or of outsiders, or of troublesome devils, and you will never see the real Buddha-nature.

At this point, if you do not cling to your state, but instead arouse your spirit to wholehearted effort, from time to time you will experience such things as forgetting you're sitting when you're sitting, forgetting you're standing when you're standing, forgetting your own body, forgetting the world around you. If you then keep going without retreating, the conscious spirit will shatter and the Buddha-nature will appear all at once. This is called the universal mirror cognition.

This is the meaning of complete perfect enlightenment at the first stage of inspiration. You can discern the source of the eighty thousand doctrines and their infinite subtle meanings all at once. As one comes into being, all come into being; as one disintegrates, all disintegrate. Nothing is lacking, no principle is not complete.

Even so, while as newborn child of Buddha the initiate enlightening being reveals the sun of wisdom of the Buddha-nature, still the clouds of habit have not yet been cleared away. Since your power in the Way is slight and your perception of reality is not perfectly clear, the universal mirror cognition is associated with the east and referred to as the gate of inspiration.

It is like the sun rising in the east; although the mountains, rivers, and land get some rays, they are not yet warmed by the sunlight. Though you see the Way clearly one day, as long as your power of shining insight is not great and strong, you are prone to hindrance by instinctual and habitual psychological afflictions, and you are still not free and independent in both pleasant and unfavorable circumstances.

This is like looking for an ox; though you may one day get to see the real ox, if you do not hold the halter firmly to keep it in check, sooner or later it will run away.

Once you see the ox, therefore, you make oxherding methods your main concern. Without such cultivation after enlightenment, many people who have seen reality miss the boat.

Therefore, cognition of equality of reality does not linger in the universal mirror cognition. Going on and on, you concentrate on cultivation in the aftermath of awakening.

First, use the intimate experience of the very essence you have seen to illumine all worlds with radiant insight. When you see something, shine through it. When you hear, shine through what you hear. Shine through your own body, sensation, perception, action, and consciousness. Shine through the six fields of sense data.

In front and in back, to the left and to the right, through every sort of upset and all kinds of downfall, enter absorption in radiant vision of the whole, seeing through all things internal and external, shining through them.

When this work becomes solid, perception of reality is perfectly clear, as clear as seeing the palm of your own hand. At this point, using this clear knowledge and insight more and more, in the midst of afflictions you shine through afflictions, in the midst of enlightenment you shine through enlightenment, in pleasant situations you shine through pleasant situations, and in unpleasant circumstances you shine through unpleasant circumstances.

When desire arises, you shine through desire. When anger arises, you shine through anger. When folly arises, you shine through folly. When the poisons of desire, anger, and folly cease to infect your mind, so that it is purified, then you shine through that pure mind.

At all times, in all places, shine through all things, be they desires or sensations, gain or loss, right or wrong, even views of Buddha and views of truth; shine through them all with your whole body. If your mind does not backslide, the nature created by your habits and actions naturally dissolves, and inconceivable liberation is realized. Then your deeds are in accord with your understanding, principle and fact merge completely, body and mind are not two, essence and appearance do not obstruct one another.

Attaining this, the realm of true equanimity, is called cognition of equality of the nature of reality.

This does not mean nondual merging into a homogenized view of formless sameness. Cognition of equality of reality refers to the point of true equanimous liberation, realized by constant refinement of your state.

Although views are equal in principle, they are not yet equal in actual fact. If you get involved in objects of old habitual conflicting emotions, your insight and power in the Way will get stuck and you won't be completely free.

Therefore, this refining cultivation after awakening is called cognition of equality of real nature, and is associated with the south and called the gate of cultivation. It is like when the sun is over the south and its light is full, illumining all hidden places in the deep ravines, drying up even hard ice and wet ground.

Even though an enlightening being has the eye to see reality, without entering this gate of cultivation it is impossible to clear away obstructions caused by emotional and intellectual baggage, and therefore impossible to attain to the state of liberation and freedom. What a pity that would be, what a loss!

Next is observing cognition. Having reached the nondual sphere of equality of true reality, it is essential at this point to attain clear understanding of the profound principles of differentiation of the enlightened ones and master techniques for helping people.

Otherwise, even if you have cultivated and attained unhindered knowledge, you will ultimately remain in the nest of the lesser vehicle and be unable to realize omniscience, unhindered knowledge, and freedom to change in any way necessary to help people; you will be unable to enlighten yourself and enlighten others, or reach the ultimate great enlightenment where awareness and action are completely perfected.

For this reason it is essential to conceive an attitude of great compassion and commitment to help all people everywhere. In order to penetrate the principles of things in their infinite variety, first you should study them day and night through the verbal teachings of the Buddhas and Zen founders.

One by one ascertaining and analyzing the profundities of the Five Houses and Seven Schools of Zen, as well as the wondrous doctrines of the Eight Teachings given in the five periods of Buddha's lifetime of teaching, if you have any energy left over you should clarify the underlying structures of the various different philosophies.

If it gets to be too much trouble to study this and that, however, it will just waste your faculties to no advantage. If you thoroughly investigate the sayings of the Buddhas and Zen founders that are difficult to penetrate, and clearly arrive at their essential import, then perfect understanding will shine forth and the patterns and principles of all things should spontaneously become clear. This is what we call the eye to read the scriptures.

Now, the verbal teachings of the Buddhas and Zen masters are extremely profound and should not be considered exhausted after you have gone through them once or twice. When you climb in the mountains, the farther you climb the higher they are; when you enter the ocean, the farther you go the deeper it is. It is the same in this case.

It is also like forging steel to make a sword: it is considered best to put it into the forge over and over, refining it again and again. Although it is always the same forge, unless you put the sword in the fire over and over and refine it a hundred times, it can hardly turn out to be a fine sword.

Penetrating study is also like this. Unless you enter the great forge of the Buddhas and Zen masters, difficult to pass through, and make repeated efforts at refinement, striving with all your might, omniscience and independent knowledge cannot emerge. Just penetrating the barrier locks of the Buddhas and Zen masters over and over again, responding to people's potentials everywhere with masterful freedom of means, is called subtle observing cognition.

This is not investigation by means of intellectual considerations. The knowledge to save oneself and the knowledge to liberate others, when completely fulfilled and mastered, are together called subtle observing cognition. This is the state of the perfectly fulfilled body of enjoyment; it is associated with the west and called the gate of enlightenment.

It is like the sun having passed high noon and gradually sinking toward the west. While the universal cognition of equality is right in the middle, you cannot perceive people's faculties and cannot clarify the teachings of differentiations among things.

If you do not stop in the realm of self-enlightenment as inner realization, but go on to cultivate this subtle observing cognition, then you have done what you can do. Having done your task, you reach the land of rest. This is not the sense of the sun setting; it has the meaning of accomplishment of all the cognitions, the fulfillment of enlightenment, because enlightening self and others, fulfillment of awareness and action, is considered real ultimate enlightenment.

Next is practical cognition. This is the secret gateway of mental command, in the realm of ultimate liberation. This is called undefiled knowledge and uncreated virtue. If you do not realize this cognition, you will not be capable of great freedom in doing what is to be done to help yourself and others.

So what is effortlessness? Because the preceding subtle observing cognition is accomplished by successful practice, and is in the realm of cultivation and realization, attainment by study, it is called knowledge with effort. This practical cognition, in contrast, transcends the bounds of practice, realization, and attainment through study; it is beyond the reach of indication and explanation.

For example, the subtle observing cognition is like the flower of complete enlightenment and practice blooming, while this practical cognition, knowledge of doing what is to be done, is like the flower of complete enlightenment and practice dropping away and the actual fruit forming. This you cannot see, even in a dream, unless you have penetrated the final transcendental pass of Zen. That is why it is said that you finally come to the unbreakable barrier at the last word.

The way to point out the direction is not in verbal explanations. If you want to reach this realm, just refine your observing cognition in the differentiated stories that are difficult to pass through, smelting and forging hundreds and thousands of times, over and over again.

Even if you have penetrated some of them, go through them over and over, examining them meticulously. What is this truth of transcendence beyond all convention? If you do not regress in your examination of the sayings of the ancients, someday you may come to know this bit of wonder.

Even so, if you do not seek an enlightened teacher and personally undergo refinement, you cannot plumb the profound subtleties. The only worry is that real Zen teachers are extremely few here and hard to find.

But if you exert your energy to the utmost in this, and penetrate through clearly, you attain freedom in all ways, transcend the realms of Buddhas and demons, and yet roam freely in the realms of Buddhas and demons, resolving sticking points, removing bonds, pulling out nails and pegs, leading people to the realm of purity and ease.

This is called practical cognition; associated with north, it is called the gate of nirvana.

It is like when the sun reaches the northern quarter, when it is midnight and the whole world is dark. When you reach the sphere of this cognition, it is not within understanding or comprehension. Even Buddhas cannot see you, much less outsiders or demons.

This is the thoroughly peaceful state of pure reality of the Buddhas and Zen masters, the forest of thorns where Zennists sit, recline, and walk around twenty-four hours a day. This is called great nirvana with four attributes—eternity, bliss, purity, and self.

It is also called cognition of the essential nature of the cosmos, in which the four cognitions are fully complete. The center has the meaning of totalizing the four knowledges, and the essential nature of the cosmos represents the sense of the enlightened one, master of teachings, being free in all ways.

I hope that Buddhists with great faith will conceive great trust and commitment and cultivate the great practice for the fulfillment of these four cognitions and true enlightenment. Don't lose out on the great matter of myriad aeons because of pride in your view of the moment.

PART THREE

ZEN KOANS

1. Buddha Takes the High Seat

Wan-sung says: "Closing the door and taking a nap is a lesson for those of highest potential. Noticing, mirroring, and stretching are details for the mediocre and the inferior. If you add to this mounting a fancy chair and sporting demon eyes, don't be surprised if a by-stander who does not agree comes forward."

> To the perceptive, there's no need to say anything; elabora-tions of teaching and practice are for those who do not experi-ence truth directly. That is why a teaching should not be evaluated by its outward appearance per se but for its total effect on an audience. Ceremonial showmanship and theatrics may pass for religion among those trained to dwell on the superficial and the contrived, but that does not mean that this is true reli-gion, or that everyone can be expected to accept it simply to avoid "rocking the boat."

One day the Buddha mounted a high seat. Manjushri, spirit of supernal wisdom, struck a signal and declared, "See in very truth the religion of the master of religion: the religion of the master of religion is 'being so.' "

Then the Buddha got down from the seat.

> The Buddha did not mount a high seat when teaching his mendicant disciples. It is only in the context of Mahayana or Universalist Buddhism that Buddha mounts a high seat, which symbolizes the seat of teaching based on a universal perspective from a point of view beyond the divisive and conflicting opinions of the world.
>
> Manjushri, the Glorious One, is one of the principal archetypi-

cal bodhisattvas, or enlightening beings, associated with the teaching of Buddha. Manjushri represents wisdom and knowledge, both transcendental and temporal. His declaration of the religion of "being so" was made before Buddha had spoken, in order to alert the audience to the immediate wholeness of universal Being So, within which the being so of every individual finds its place in an infinitely rich nexus of relations.

Since there was nothing more to say—for indeed the religion of being so is only understood by being so—Buddha said nothing and immediately got down from the high seat.

And there is another reason why Buddha "descended," to show that after awakening (which is what "Buddha" represents), each of us has to "descend" from the experience of universal Being So to the experience of individual responsibility for being so. The purpose and meaning of awakening is in the essential link between universal Being So and individual being so. To learn to maintain and safeguard this connection consciously in the midst of the everyday world is the "descending from the high seat" and resumption of individual responsibility on the highest level even in the lowly estate of earthly existence. This is also why Buddha may be depicted, at one level of tradition, as wearing "rags" even after attainment of Buddhahood, symbolizing his conscious resumption of temporal human existence in the world after attainment of release.

T'ien-t'ung said in verse:

A gust of reality—do you see?
Continuously the mother of evolution runs her loom and shuttle,
Weaving an ancient brocade containing the forms of spring,
Nothing to do with the leaking evinced by the Eastern Lord.

The gust of reality is "being so." Do you see? This is not a superficial question. Being as is, like Creation weaving a timeless tapestry, is no more and no less for being illustrated or described.

The Eastern Lord is Manjushri, the personification of knowledge. True reality is really there whether or not we are aware of it, whether or not we discuss it or define it. Discussions and definitions, in fact, may only serve to obscure the immediate reality. A Zen proverb says, "Ordinary people use it every day, but without knowing."

2. Emptiness

Wan-sung says: "Someone who presented a jewel in the matrix three times to a king did not escape punishment. Thrown a luminous pearl, few are those who do not react defensively. There may be a sudden guest, but not a sudden host; what may be suitable temporarily is not suitable in reality. If rarities and treasures cannot be used, bring forth something whose price can't be named."

A teaching may not be visible to one who seeks through outward appearances. Even the most valuable piece of advice may be rejected when it comes in an unexpected manner or form. Seekers approach a source of teaching with all sorts of arbitrary expectations, but a real teacher does not indulge these subjective imaginings; to communicate at all, it may be necessary to find a common convention, but this is only a provisional means, not an actual end. Drama and excitement are useless when it comes to objective perception of reality, an experience so truly unique that "no one can name its price."

Emperor Wu of Liang asked the great teacher Bodhidharma, "What is the ultimate meaning of the holy truths?"
Bodhidharma replied, "Empty, without holiness."
The emperor said, "Who is in my presence?"
Bodhidharma answered, "Don't know."

The emperor didn't get it, so Bodhidharma crossed over the Long River. Coming to Shaolin, he faced a wall for nine years.

Sometimes people wishing to follow Buddhism cannot really accept being so, and instead dress up in costumes and play charades. All the supposed sanctity of pious fools and pretended seekers is but so much vanity and illusion.

Bodhidharma is thought of as the founder of Zen in China. Cutting through scholastic and ceremonial showmanship, eschewing politics dressed in religious garb, he pointed directly to the ineffable essence of awakening, which is traditionally said to be like the knife that cuts but does not cut itself, like the eye that sees but does not see itself. That is why the teacher says, "Don't know" when the emperor asks him who he is.

Seeing as how the emperor does not understand the essential, the teacher knows he cannot teach him any more than this; so he leaves the emperor's domain. Buddhism cannot be bought or sold.

Facing a wall stands for immovability of mind attained through realization of the universal essence of consciousness. Nine years represents the nine time frames of the past, present, and future of the past, present, and future. Directly experiencing the essential nature of the absolute that is empty of all imaginary constructions and unchanged throughout all time is the fundamental way of Zen.

T'ien-t'ung said in verse:

Empty, without holiness—the approach is way off.
The success is like swinging an ax without causing injury;
The failure is like dropping a pitcher without looking back.
Quietly sitting cool at Shaolin,
Silently he expressed the true order.
Autumn's clear moon turns its frosty disk;
Milky Way thin, the Dipper lowers its handle in the night.

The robe and bowl of the lineage are handed to successors;
From this people have made both medicine and disease.

> The emperor's expectations of something grandiose were dashed by the teacher shattering his pious conceptions.
>
> The teacher's success was in undermining an illusion without injury to real potential. The teacher did not let failure to enable the emperor to understand tempt him to engage in compromise or cajolery; having dropped the pitcher, he knew there was no point in looking back.
>
> Quietly sitting cool means being just so, without telling yourself stories or giving yourself pep rallies. This is what expresses the fundamental truth of the fabricated nature of our subjective conceptions of ourselves and the world.
>
> The clarity of unvarnished truth is "cold," admitting of no sentimentality. Only when the stream of consciousness is free of clinging thoughts does the mystery become accessible to the mind's eye.
>
> While forms and methods of liberating techniques have been handed on since time immemorial, their efficacy depends on how they are used. For the truthful they can be medicine, but the obsessive turn them into disease.

3. Invitation of a Patriarch

Wan-sung says: "The unmanifested potential before time—a black tortoise turns toward fire. The unique statement separately transmitted outside of dogma—the edge of a mortar blooms with flowers. Tell me, is there any accepting and upholding, reading and reciting?"

> The black tortoise stands for the absolute state, which in Zen is called the heart of nirvana; turning toward a fire represents the

turning point of the Zen stages known as coming from within the absolute and arriving within the relative.

The unique statement separately transmitted outside dogma refers to the experience of direct perception, which cannot be described in words or defined in concepts. The edge of a mortar blooming with flowers represents the inconceivable activity of the life potential working spontaneously, appearing as if miraculously to the uncontrived heart of nirvana.

How can artificial practices capture this state?

A king of east India invited the twenty-seventh patriarch Prajnatara to a vegetarian meal. The king asked, "Why don't you read scriptures?"

The patriarch said, "When breathing in I do not dwell in the clusters and elements of body and mind; when breathing out I do not get involved in any objects. I continually recite this scripture—hundreds, thousands, millions of scrolls."

There are many concentration exercises involving coordination of breathing and attention. Many pseudo-Zen cults teach people to count their breaths and call this zazen or meditation, but concentration without insight is dangerous in that it actually hardens the shell of the ego and concentrates psychological pollutants rather than removing them.

It might be supposed that the Buddhist patriarch—Prajnatara was thought to have been the teacher of Bodhidharma, founder of Zen in China—was illustrating a method of mindfulness of the breathing. But look at the disposition of his attention—can it be said that he is practicing mindfulness of breathing? Is he mindful or not? Of what is he mindful? This exercise is a lot more subtle than it seems at a glance; that is why Wan-sung has us ask if it is susceptible to formulation and transmission or can only be realized by direct experience.

94

T'ien-t'ung said in verse:

A cloud rhino enjoys the moonlight, radiance full of brilliance;
A wooden horse frolics in spring, fleet and unfettered.
Below the brows, a pair of cold green eyes;
How can scripture reading come to pierce ox hide?
A clear clean mind produces immense aeons,
Heroic virile power smashes a double enclosure.
The spiritual mechanism is made to pivot
In the opening of subtle roundness.
One forgot the road along which he came;
The other led him back, taking him by the hand.

> The cloud rhino and wooden horse are the true potential latent within the human mind; enjoying the moon and frolicking in spring represent the true potential released, no longer bound to objects.
>
> The green eyes refer to the Buddhist patriarch. In Chinese Zen, people from the West—Central Asia and the Indian subcontinent—are sometimes referred to as having blue or green eyes. This is based on the startling impression caused on the Chinese people of the early centuries of the Common Era by the appearance of Central Asian Buddhists with green or gray eyes. The patriarch's eyes are "cold" in that he sees reality without embellishment and he therefore refuses to regale the king with a show.
>
> Piercing ox hide refers to penetrating insight, which cannot be obtained by the discursive intellect alone but also requires the awakening of direct perception, referred to in the Buddhist Sanskrit of the patriarch as *pratyaksha-pramana* or *pratyaksha-darshana*. Reading scriptures in an academic manner does not employ or arouse this direct experience; they must be read in the Buddhist way, with the totality of the being. That is why the verse poses it as a question—how can scripture reading come to

piercing ox hide? We ourselves are asked to differentiate formality from actuality, conceptual reading from experiential reading.

The clear clean mind producing aeons represents the expansiveness of the experience of mind liberated from dependence on objects. Heroic power smashing the double enclosure depicts the patriarch's practice of resting attention neither on internal objects nor on external objects, mental or physical, abstract or concrete.

The opening of subtle roundness seems like the mechanism of breathing, but in reality it is the subtle space of uninhibited awareness, which allows the spiritual mechanism of attention to operate freely.

The one who forgot the road along which he came is the king, who is alienated by his preconceptions from direct perception of natural reality, the source of everything, and thus is seeking something special as "religious practice." The one who took him by the hand to lead him back is the patriarch, who returns attention to the recondite pivotal point of freedom, and does so in an uncomplicated manner, as simply and directly as leading someone by the hand.

4. Buddha Points to the Ground

Wan-sung says: "The moment one particle is brought up, the whole earth is contained in it. Who is it that can open the borders and extend the land as a lone rider with a single lance, and so can be the master anywhere and encounter the source in everything?"

If everything is interdependent, then everything is part of the existence of every thing. Using this one quintessential understanding of universal interdependence, it is possible to extend the horizons of consciousness by means of the infinite network of causality. In this way, we are in the midst of the limitless even in the midst of the finite; what determines the depth and breadth of our world is the richness or poverty of our perception.

Once as the Buddha was walking along with a group, he pointed to the ground and said, "This place is suitable for building a sanctuary."

Shakra, Emperor of Angels, stuck a blade of grass in the ground and declared, "The building of the sanctuary is done."

The Buddha smiled.

Buddha traveled in the company of all beings. Shakra, the Emperor of Angels, is also called Indra. In the Avatamsaka teaching, the pearl net of Indra in the skies above reflecting the world below represents the infinite network of interdependent phenomena and principles.

Buddha points at the ground and says it is suitable for a sanctuary; this stands for the universal principle, which is everywhere. Indra plants a blade of grass in the ground and declares the sanctuary built; this stands for the concrete manifestation of principle in phenomena. Realizing the perfect correspondence of the abstract and the concrete is the third of four realms of reality in Avatamsaka Buddhism and the third of five ranks in the Ts'ao-Tung school of Ch'an Buddhism.

T'ien-t'ung said in verse:

Infinite spring in the hundred grasses;
Picked up in what comes to hand, it's used familiarly.
The glorious embodiment of virtuous qualities,
Leisurely Buddha leads by the hand into the red dust,
Able to be master in the dust;
A visitor shows up from outside Creation,
Life enough as it is wherever he is,
Not minding if he's not as clever as others.

The infinite spring in the hundred grasses is the universal principle underlying phenomena. When this universal principle is realized, it can be illustrated in anything.

An embodiment of virtuous qualities represents Buddha as embodying abstract truth in concrete manifestations. The practice of enlightenment is actualized in the ordinary world, while the enlightenment of the practitioner is independent of objects.

The Emperor of Angels is the guest from outside Creation. The idea of being "outside Creation" in this case refers to a total perspective on the whole of being, rather than a limited perspective from an isolated point of view. The sufficiency of his life wherever he is refers to his ability to experience everything as part of everything else; unconcern for his comparative lack of cleverness refers to the actual reality of universal interdependence, which does not need to be artificially constructed to be true.

5. The Price of Rice

Wan-sung says: "Siddhartha gouged out his own flesh to feed his parents, but this is not listed in legends of devoted children; Devadatta pushed over a mountain to crush Buddha, but he did not fear a sudden thunderclap, did he? Passing through a forest of thorns, cutting down a sandalwood tree, when the year is ended, early spring is still cold as ever; where is the reality body of Buddhas?"

Siddhartha is the name of Gautama Buddha before his renunciation of worldly status. Devadatta was Siddhartha's cousin, who shamelessly opposed Buddha and is named as an arch enemy of Buddhism. Siddhartha's act of devotion does not appear in secular records; a good deed does not need to be made known. Devadatta was unrepentant in his treachery; an evil deed may not be recognized by oneself.

Passing through a forest of thorns means dealing with life as it is; cutting down a sandalwood tree means getting over pious fantasies. When you finish dreaming, reality is as ever; it's not that it was somewhere else and suddenly shows up.

Someone asked Ch'ing-yuan, "What is the great meaning of Buddhism?"

Ch'ing-yuan said, "What is the price of rice in the city?"

The price of rice is "being so." Even knowing this, it is still necessary to ask what Buddhism means and what the price of food is; it is necessary to understand ultimate truth and conditional truth together, neither confusing them nor alienating them. If you think a fixed answer is understanding, you don't even know the prices in your own town.

T'ien-t'ung said in verse:

The work of the government of Halcyon is formless;
The manners of the old rustics are pure and pristine.
All they know is village songs and festival parties;
What do they care about the virtues of ancient kings?

This verse is about noncontrivance, nothing more; that is the window to being so, the price of rice in the city. There is a Zen proverb that says, "A false doctrine is hard to uphold." This means that hoked-up complications are inherently toilsome, no matter how colorfully dressed or dramatically rehearsed. Only vain careerists would bother with such artificialities; only vain dreamers would put up with them.

99

6. White and Black

Wan-sung says: "When nothing can be said, a tongueless man can speak; where not a step can be taken, a legless man can walk. If you fall within the range of another and stagnate at a statement, how can you have any independence? When the elements oppress you, how can you penetrate to liberty?"

A tongueless man represents someone who has no rigid fixations of thought habit; such a person can understand and express what is not accessible to conventional thinking. A legless man is one who does not depend on anything; such a person can go where there is no support for dependence.

How can this freedom be attained if you remain within the limits imposed by another? How can liberty be realized if you turn everything into a cliché? How can you be emancipated when everything weighs on your mind?

A seeker asked Grand Master Ma, "Leaving aside all possible propositions, please give me a direct indication of the meaning of living Buddhism."

The grand master said, "I'm tired today; I can't explain it to you. Go ask Chih Tsang."

The seeker asked Chih Tsang, who said, "Why not ask the teacher?"

The seeker replied, "The teacher told me to come ask you."

Chih Tsang said, "I have a headache today; I can't explain it to you. Go ask brother Hai."

The seeker asked Hai. Hai said, "At this point, I don't understand."

The seeker related all this to the grand master. The grand master said, "Tsang's head is white, Hai's head is black."

This seeker wanted to go beyond logical understanding to direct experience. The grand master showed him how without fur-

ther ado, but the seeker didn't understand, so the master's enlightened disciple Tsang repeated the lesson. The seeker still
didn't understand, so another one of the master's enlightened
disciples, the one named Hai, showed him that this kind of realization is not the same thing as a conceptual understanding.

The master says that the first disciple's head is white, for he
gives his lesson in terms of the temporal, conditional world, while
the second disciple's head is black, as he gives his lesson in reference to the inconceivable absolute. Complete Zen realization
encompasses both the conditional and the absolute, without either confusion or contradiction.

T'ien-t'ung said in verse:

Medicine causing sickness is shown up by the ancient sages;
For sickness to be medicine, who does it require?
White head and black head are capable heirs of the house;
Statement and no statement are devices to cut off the flow.
Commanding majesty stopping the road of speech,
Laughable the silent Buddha of old.

Medicine causing sickness refers to confusing oneself by thinking subjectively about the principles of the Buddhist teaching.
The ancient sages show this by illustrating flaws and gaps of understanding. In order for a seeker to awaken by being shown the
error of his or her ways, it is necessary to have someone with
objective vision, as well as a flexible and receptive attitude on
the part of the seeker.

The relative and the absolute are both part of Zen experience;
the manifest and the unmanifest are both vehicles of realization.
Attention might be drawn to the concrete to interrupt preoccupation with abstractions; conversely, attention might be shifted
to the abstract to interrupt preoccupation with the concrete.

The silent Buddha of old refers to Vimalakirti, a lay Buddha,
famed for his silent reply to a question about entry into nondual-

ity. His silence is called laughable so people will not imitate it
falsely, trying to disguise ignorance as wisdom, and so people
will not become obsessed with an exaggerated conception of the
absolute as being like utter silence and nothingness.

7. Taking the High Seat

Wan-Sung says: "The eyes, ears, nose, and tongue each have a capacity, while the eyebrows remain above; warriors, farmers, craftsmen,
and merchants each have a job, while the unskilled are always at
leisure. How does a real teacher of the source set up devices?"

> The functions of the senses and the occupational classes rep-
> resent the realm of action and effort, while the eyebrows and the
> unskilled stand for noncontrivance and effortlessness. One may
> begin by striving, but until one attains nonstriving the reality of
> being so does not become clear.

Once when Yao-shan had not taken the high seat for a long time,
the abbot of the temple said to him, "The group has been wishing
for instruction for a long time; please give them a lecture on the
teaching."

So Yao-shan had the bell rung, and took the high seat when the
group had gathered. After a long silence, he got off the seat and went
back to his quarters.

The abbot followed after him, asking, "You just agreed to expound
the teaching to the group; why didn't you say anything?"

Yao-shan said, "There are professors of scripture for scriptures,
there are professors of treatises for treatises; how can you blame me?"

> The real teaching is not a string of words, it is the experience
> of reality itself. When people are conditioned to receiving
> "teaching" in preconceived forms and formulas, they cease to

actually learn from this "teaching." Those who fall into this habit are rehearsing clichés, not studying reality. Unless they have gone too far, they may be roused from their slumber by a lesson like that given by the master Yao-shan.

T'ien-t'ung said in verse:

A silly baby bothers over "money" used to stop crying;
A good horse chases the wind, noticing the shadow of the whip.
Clouds sweep the eternal sky; nesting in the moon, a crane,
Cold clarity gone into his bones, such that he cannot sleep.

"Money" to stop crying is a classical representation of Buddhist teachings, which are setups devised to stop delusion. According to a scriptural story, a mother holds a handful of yellow leaves out to a crying child, saying that she will give him this "money" if he stops crying. That means the teachings are liberative expedients, not binding dogma.

So Master Yao-shan offers the abbot a lecture to stop his whining. Although he said nothing, a "good horse," that is, a quick learner, would get the message at once. A quick learner is said to be like a good horse who gallops off at the mere shadow of the whip and does not need to actually be struck. Likewise, a sharp student would get the silent message of Yao-shan's unspoken "lecture" and would not need a lot of talk.

The eternal sky is the eternal void, the ungraspable, inconceivable ground of reality. Clouds sweeping the eternal sky are the transitory events of the conditional world, whose very ephemerality is always demonstrating the emptiness of eternity. The moon stands for awareness of the absolute, the "high seat" Yao-shan takes up, which is so "cold," so void of sentimental attachment to familiar habits of thought, that one cannot fall into the sleep of conventional cliché. This represents Yao-shan refusing to entertain the troops; his aim was to enlighten them, not amuse them.

8. A Wild Fox

Wan-sung says: "If you keep so much as the dot of an *i* in your mind, you go to hell like an arrow shot; if you swallow even a drop of wild fox slobber, you won't be able to spit it out for thirty years. It's not that the order in India is strict but that the ignoramus is weighed down with compulsive habit. Has there ever been anyone who didn't make a mistake?"

> Buddhist teachings are not for memorizing and spewing out to others at the drop of a hat. If you memorize a bunch of slogans and clichés, thinking this to be enlightenment, you will only become more unbearable to yourself and others; if you swallow the drivel of false teachers who delude others by taking advantage of irresponsibility and wishful thinking, it will stick to your ribs and keep you stuffed.
>
> This is not a matter of dogmatic principle but of natural reality. If you are fixated on preconceived ideas, your attention has no room for anything else; as long as you are full of self-congratulating rationalizations, your mental faculties cannot digest and absorb anything of objective truth.
>
> Has there ever been anyone who never made a mistake? If you think this excuses mistakes, you are mistaken.

Whenever Pai-chang talked in the auditorium, there was always an old man listening to the teaching. He usually left with the crowd, but one day he didn't go. Pai-chang then asked him who he was.

"I used to live on this mountain in the remote past, in the time of Kashyapa Buddha," explained the old man, "when a student asked me whether or not greatly cultivated people are still subject to causality. I replied that they are not subject to causality, and deteriorated into an embodiment of a wild fox for five hundred lifetimes. Now I ask you to turn a word for me."

Pai-chang said, "Not blind to causality."

At these words, the old man was greatly enlightened.

The idea of Buddhist practice as a way to escape from problems without facing them or understanding them is one that appeals to the greedy and the lazy. The idea of liberty as freedom from responsibility is one that appeals to the reckless and the aggressive. Those who offer hypertensive meditation intensives to all and sundry, as if they were going to have some sort of spiritual experience in a few days, are covertly appealing not to spiritual aspirations but to the greed, laziness, recklessness, and aggressiveness commonly found within emotionally and intellectually immature and irresponsible adults.

Often such people will perform, or put on performances, of ritualized exercises at regular intervals, and eventually delude themselves into unconsciously thinking, without saying so, that they are transcendentally justified and are not subject to ordinary causality. The same master as in this story, the great Pai-chang, also said, "That which the power of concentration holds eventually leaks out to regenerate in another domain, totally unawares."

That is why people who are in fact highly cultivated are "not blind to causality."

T'ien-t'ung said in verse:

A foot of water, a fathom of wave,
Helpless for five hundred lives.
Whether you say not subject
Or you say not blind,
You're still haggling your way
Into a nest of complications.
Ah, ha, ha! Do you understand?
If you are free, untrammeled,
You won't mind my babble.
Sacred songs and shrine dances
Form a harmony of their own,
Clapping to the intervals and singing liltingly.

A foot of water may be a word, an act, or a thought. The fathom of wave is the total complex of results and consequences emanating from a single event. A foot of water and a fathom of wave thus can also mean, in a specialized sense, practice and realization. Being helpless for five hundred lifetimes refers to what is called horizontal emancipation, working one's way through the world without a sense of "doing" anything. The consequences of denying causality, in the case of the old man who became a fox, were "five hundred lifetimes" of events, showing him the practical necessity of not being blind to causality.

The question of free will is not a theoretical issue. Even if one can master one's own behavior, one cannot necessarily control the total environment and therefore cannot necessarily control all the effects and consequences caused by and resulting from one's behavior. The degree to which one can escape subjection to causality depends, therefore, on the degree to which one can overcome ignorance of causality.

Thus an academic argument between "not subject" and "not blind," as if these were dogmatically polarized "positions," would still lead nowhere but into a nest of complications, not to liberation and enlightenment.

If we want to perceive causality objectively, we cannot do so just by sticking to preconceived notions of cause and effect. Only when we are "clear and free" of distorting and limited preconceptions can we discern the real meanings in events.

Once we are able to discern in this way, we find the laws of natural reality working themselves out on their own, in their own ways. We are already a part of these goings-on; the question is whether or not we are conscious and responsible participants. We do not need to varnish the works with fixed ideas and rigid dogma; what we need to do is learn to keep up with the rhythm of reality and attune ourselves to its harmony.

9. Killing a Cat

Wan-sung says: "Kick over the ocean, and dust flies on earth. Scatter the clouds with a shout, and the sky itself shatters. Strict execution of the absolute imperative is still but half the matter; how is the total manifestation of the greater potential set up?"

> Inner mental changes cause outward behavioral changes. When you stop projecting, conflicts based on disparities in subjective perceptions disappear.
>
> People who seek what they imagine to be liberation or enlightenment out of laziness suppose that all they have to do is attain an experience of the absolute and all their problems will be solved for all time. Few things could be further from the truth.
>
> In the first place, such people never even glimpse the true absolute. They wind up seeking intoxication in trance or slumber in ceremonial habit. This is called "neither getting to the shop ahead, nor reaching the village behind."
>
> It is essential to realize the transcendence of the absolute and to understand the relativity of the temporal. An ancient master said, "First go over to the Beyond, to know that it exists; then come back to the here-and-now to act." Wan-sung said, "It is comparatively easy to attain the heart of nirvana, harder to clarify the knowledge of differentiation."

One day the eastern and western groups at Nan-ch'uan's were having a dispute about a cat. Seeing this, Nan-ch'uan picked up the cat and said, "If you can speak, I won't kill it."

Nobody had a response.

Nan-ch'uan killed the cat, cutting it in two.

Subsequently Nan-ch'uan told Chao-chou this story and asked him about it. Chao-chou immediately doffed his straw sandals and walked out wearing them on his head.

Nan-ch'uan said, "Had you been here, you would have saved the cat."

The cat stands for everything; Wan-sung says, "At that moment all beings in the whole universe, animate and inanimate, are there together in Nan-ch'uan's hands, begging for their lives."

The *Flower Ornament Scripture* says, "Beings teach, lands teach, all things in all times teach, constantly, without interruption." Disputation is not the way to hear this teaching; while your emotions and your intellect are arguing back and forth, reality passes you by, as you "stumble past without being aware of it."

This situation makes a burden of what should be a protection. Emotions and intelligence are like shoes, which enable us to walk, to act efficiently, by cushioning us from the impact of the world at large. Emotion cushions us by alerting us to instinctive feelings of attraction and danger, while intelligence cushions us by enabling us to make sense of an otherwise chaotic world. Putting these shoes on the head rather than the feet means letting emotion and intelligence represent the ego rather than making them tools of the real self, which is essential Buddha-nature. A similar case could be made for the relationship between intuition and reason. The divisive course leads to argumentation, while the other, integration from a higher perspective, leads to resolution.

T'ien-t'ung said in verse:

Two groups of wanderers, all in a brawl;
The teacher could tell right from wrong.
The sharp knife cut through, regardless of form,
Endearing people forever to a real adept.
This Path has not died out;
A connoisseur is to be appreciated.
Only King Yu could drain the Flood,
Only Lady Wa could mend the sky.
Old Chao-chou had a life;
He got somewhere with sandals on his head.

His difference from the others is clearly evident;
This is the real gold that isn't mixed with sand.

This verse just describes the story. The connoisseur to be appreciated is Chao-chou. King Yu, the hero of ancient history who dug sluices to save China from the great Flood, stands for Nan-ch'uan. Lady Wa, an even more ancient culture hero who repaired the sky after the pillar of heaven broke, represents Chao-chou. The last four lines are all about Chao-chou. In Zen parlance, to have a life means to return to the ordinary from the pinnacle of transcendence; he "got somewhere with sandals on his head" in the sense that this act was not a piece of nonsense but an ordinary demonstration of mirroring folly to let people see themselves. Thus Chao-chou was transcendent in being beyond the disputation, yet not blind to it and not lacking in compassion, insofar as he sacrificed his own dignity to show others how confused they were. Although in the midst of this confusion Chao-chou is not confused; although he does not ignore the dispute, he does not enter into it. This is the gold that is not mixed with sand.

10. The Woman of T'ai-shan

Wan-sung says: "Whether gathering in or letting go, he always has his equipment with him; able to kill and able to give life, the balance is in his hands. Mundane toils, demons, and outsiders all rely on his direction; the mountains and rivers of the whole earth are his playthings. What realm is this?"

Gathering in and letting go are Ch'an terms for being inaccessible and being accommodating; a real master is able to gather in and let go according to the requirements of the situation, always having this "equipment" or ability at the ready. Killing and giving life are parallel terms used with reference to the absolute and the relative; the absolute "kills" delusion, the relative "gives life" to knowledge. The balance of these complementary operations of Ch'an mind is in the hands of the adept.

When you have reached this level of mastery, you are able to make use of everything in an enlightening way, even confusion; unaffected by the excitement and the lull of the world, you are able to participate freely and independently. But how do you test for the authenticity of this realm of experience?

There was a certain woman who lived on the road to the sacred mountain T'ai-shan. Whenever a mendicant asked her which way the road to T'ai-shan was, the woman would say, "Straight ahead." Then as soon as the mendicant would head off, the woman would say, "A fine cleric! And so he goes!"

A mendicant told Chao-chou about this. Chao-chou said, "Wait till I have tested her."

Chao-chou asked the woman the same question. The next day he declared, "I have tested the woman for you."

Ch'an masters did not encourage people to make pilgrimages to sacred mountains or holy sites. "Gazing at the moon in the sky," the Ch'an proverb goes, "you lose the pearl in your hand."

Asked about the route to the sacred mountain, the woman answered about the route to being so: "Straight ahead."

The woman's followup remark, "And so he goes," is a way of checking to see how the questioner understood the answer.

When a mendicant told the great Ch'an master Chao-chou about this, he may have been wondering about the woman, or he may have been testing Chao-chou himself. In response, Chao-chou both tested and taught the mendicant, showing him how it is done.

If you think something is missing from this story, you haven't done your own checking. This is not a quip, or a conundrum, but a reference to what is wanting; that is not in the story, but it is not missing from the story. The story is complete, and yet something is wanting. That is you doing your own checking. That is the message of Chao-chou's trip.

T'ien-t'ung said in verse:

Mellowing to perfection, not transmitting in error,
Chao-chou the old Buddha succeeded to Nan-ch'uan.
The dead tortoise's demise was due to designs on its shell;
The swiftest steeds are encumbered by halter and bridle.
When you have checked the woman's Ch'an,
It's not worth a cent to tell it to others.

The first two lines eulogize Chao-chou. His teacher Nan-ch'uan was famous for undermining all fixations, especially religious fixations masquerading as true spirituality.

The second two lines continue the eulogy in specific terms. The idea that tortoises are killed because people want their shells for their own purposes, and that powerful horses are bridled because people want their speed for their own purposes, is a way of stating the Buddhist ideal of freedom, represented by way of contrast. These lines also specifically praise the freedom from complications in Chao-chou's response to the mendicant's inquiry.

The last two lines focus even more specifically on the nature and content of Chao-chou's response, demonstrating the pragmatic beauty of its understatement and subtlety. The reason why it is not worth a cent told to others has nothing to do with the woman, except for T'ien-t'ung's mischievous test of you all to see whether you thought it did. The reason it is not worth a cent told to others is that you have to see for yourself. That is what Chao-chou showed us. Old as he was, he still went to see for himself. Now it's our turn.

11. Two Sicknesses

Wan-sung says: "When the bodiless suffer illness, the handless compound medicine; the mouthless take it, the senseless get well. But what about a mortal disease—how do you treat it?"

> The illness of the bodiless is illusion, which is ultimately unreal; the medicine compounded by the handless is liberative teaching technique not held to as dogma. The mouthless taking medicine is applying the teaching without taking it in as an object in itself; the senseless getting well means awakening without attachment to the idea or feeling of awakening.
>
> What about a mortal disease? The question, based on the foregoing description of Buddhist "healing," is what constitutes "disease" and what makes it "mortal" in the first place. Asking yourself this question amounts to asking yourself how it feels to be. Not how you feel, but how it feels to be.

The great teacher Yun-men said, "When illumination does not penetrate to liberation, there are two kinds of sickness.

"One is when it is not clear everywhere, and there is something before you.

"When you have managed to penetrate the emptiness of all phenomena, yet there subtly seems to be something there, this too is failure of illumination to penetrate to liberation.

"The absolute, furthermore, also has two kinds of sickness. One is when you have reached the absolute but your personal view is still there because you haven't let go of absolutist fixation, and so you become trapped in the realm of absolutism.

"Even if you pass through, it will not do if you let mistakes go; keep examining to see if there is any breath there, for this too is a sickness."

> Certain psychological experiences may lead people to believe they have attained transcendental liberation, yet when push

comes to shove they are still obstructed by existence. Thus it is said that the light of illumination does not penetrate freely. People who concentrate intensely for too long without incisive insight often contract a "sickness" like this. Ch'an master Mi-an, who lived centuries after Yun-men, also reported such a phenomenon: "Just because of never having personally realized awakening, people temporarily halt sensing of objects, then take the bit of light that appears before their eyes to be the ultimate. This is most miserable."

Fixation on absolutism is another common defect to be seen in deteriorated Buddhist practice. Here the original term *fa-shen* or *dharmakaya* is used in the sense of "nirvana," one of its principal meanings in classical Buddhist terminology. Attachment to the peace of nirvana, or to the feeling "I have attained nirvana," is a part of what is known in Zen as the religious ego; it is, of course, not real nirvana in the true sense of the word.

But even if one does break through to absolute nirvana, it is still an illusion to imagine one is thereby purged of all impulses of habit energy. Such an experience may delude one into thinking one can no longer make any mistakes, so it is wrong to let go with relief. Now one must examine for even the slightest breath of the minutest stirrings of grasping and compulsion, because this is a sickness, a source of suffering.

T'ien-t'ung said in verse:

The totality of forms is so steep,
But passing through to infinity blocks the eyes.
Who has the strength to sweep out his garden?
Hidden in human hearts, it turns into feelings.
A boat crosses a rustic ford, steeped in the azure of autumn,
Rowing into the reed flowers reflecting the light off the snow.
An old fisherman with a bolt of silk takes it to the market;
Floating lightly in the wind, a single leaf traverses the waves.

The totality of forms is steep, but passing through to infinity blocks the eyes; this means that the way of the true Buddhist is through the world, not avoiding its difficulties, not plunging into oblivion in the absolute.

Who has the strength to sweep out his garden? The emptiness of the absolute is not realized by rejecting or denying things, or by trying to blank the mind.

Hidden in human hearts, it turns into feelings; if you become fixated upon "emptiness" as a principle or as a state of mind, this gives the sense of something there, which obstructs penetrating illumination of insight.

A boat crossing a rustic ford steeped in the azure of autumn refers to stagnation in the stillness of the absolute; rowing into the reed flowers reflecting the light off the snow refers to being dazzled by direct perception of the absolute. Wan-sung quotes, "When pure light shines in your eyes, it seems you have missed your home; turning around in pure clarity, you fall into that state."

The last two lines describe what is known as "entering the marketplace with hands extended," transcending transcendence to reenter the ordinary world, "not avoiding the wind and waves," neither reifying nor denying things, realizing the nonresistance of the absolute without making that into an object either, being in the world but not of the world, free to come and go. Wan-sung says, "With his own sickness cured, he takes pity on the ailments of others." Yet he cautions, "With many ailments, you learn about medicines; but only if it gets results do you dare pass on a prescription." Beware of leeches!

12. Planting the Fields

Wan-sung says: "Scholars plow with the pen, orators plow with the tongue. We who practice Ch'an lazily watch a white ox on clear ground, paying no attention to the auspicious grasses without roots. How do you pass the days?"

The white ox on clear ground is a scriptural symbol for suchness, the universal and individual practice of being so. To watch over this "lazily" means to be always mindful of being as is without becoming inwardly frantic or obsessed with the idea of being so. Paying no attention to rootless auspicious grasses means not becoming enthused by extraordinary experiences that occur along the journey. How do you pass the days? This is solved by how you pass the days, not by how you talk about passing the days.

Ti-tsang asked Hsiu-shan, "Where have you come from?"
Hsiu-shan said, "From the South."
Ti-tsang asked, "How is Buddhism in the South these days?"
Hsiu-shan said, "There's a lot of discussion."
Ti-tsang remarked, "How can that compare to me here planting the fields and making rice balls to eat?"
Hsiu-shan asked, "What about the mundane?"
Ti-tsang retorted, "What are you calling mundane?"

Buddhists have a saying that "there is nothing true of the world that is not true in Buddhism, and there is nothing true of Buddhism that is not true of the world." It is also said, "If you are not sentimental about them, things of the world become Buddhist teachings; if you are sentimental about them, Buddhist teachings become worldly things."

The *Diamond Sutra* says, "Buddhism is not Buddha's Teaching." Gathering groupies and coteries of so-called Buddhists talking a lot about their supposed Buddhism is not what Buddha taught. What Buddha taught was to live without illusion. How can a lot of blabber compare to constructive activity? If you think life as it is is mundane, what are you calling mundane? What do you think life is? Why do you think of it so mundanely? Ti-tsang, whose name means "Treasury of the Earth," has us ask ourselves all of these questions, if we want to know the actual truth as it is.

T'ien-t'ung said in verse:

Sects and doctrines are all made up;
Second-hand transmission fails already from ear to mouth.
Planting the fields and making rice balls are ordinary chores,
But only those who've studied fully are the ones who know;
Having studied fully, they clearly know there's nothing to seek.
The victorious warrior doesn't care to be enfeoffed as a lord;
Mindless of opportunity, he returns, like the fish and birds,
To wash his feet in the river, the hazy autumn waters.

Being so is described as ordinariness, but this does not mean the ordinariness of the unregenerate man. It is only after realization of the purpose of religion and doctrine that we can attain to the reality to which religion and doctrine are designed to lead; and only after that can we see what it means to say that religions and doctrines are all made up.

Yet even while we need the tools afforded by religions and doctrines to orient our mental activity toward reality, we cannot regard the reality of religion and doctrine to be repetitive dissemination, automatic passing on from ear to mouth to ear to mouth. There are some things we all must do for ourselves; as the Dhammapada says, the enlightened only show the way. We have to do our own work and take our own responsibilities; only after we have put true principles into true practice do we harmonize with objective reality. Then and only then are we home free, so to speak; only then do we realize there is nothing to seek, because reality is right there teaching us all along. But we only know this when we know it, and can only act on it when we act on it.

And that knowledge and action is not the same thing as profession and fanfare, not the same thing as preaching and activism. "They enter the water without making a ripple," says the proverb, depicting those who have achieved mastery of themselves, mingling inconspicuously with the Life at large in all its multifarious manifestations, modestly fulfilling their own unique roles of being what they are.

13. The Blind Ass

Wan-sung says: "When completely absorbed in helping others, you're not aware of yourself. You should exert the law to the utmost, without concern that there be no populace; you need to have the ruthless ability to snap a block of wood. What should you do when about to go?"

If you lend a helping hand to another so that you yourself can feel virtuous or superior, or so that another will be grateful or indebted to you, then you are not really helping another. Holding back truth for your own sentimental reasons—such as fear of personal rejection or hostility—is not the way to help people who are in fact seeking truth and not seeking to be mollified.

Quite a bit of Ch'an teaching involves dealing with seekers' responses to unfamiliar impacts. When a teacher is about to pass away, and therefore will no longer be on hand to monitor and adjust students' reactions and interpretations, what should be done to leave an enduring lesson?

When Lin-chi was about to pass away, he instructed San-sheng, "After my passing, don't destroy my treasury of perception of truth."

San-sheng responded, "How dare I destroy the teacher's treasury of perception of truth?"

Lin-chi asked, "If someone questions you about it, how will you answer?"

San-sheng shouted.

Lin-chi said, "Who would have known that my treasury of perception of truth would die out with this blind ass!"

> The heart of Ch'an Buddhism is referred to as a subtlety that cannot be transmitted, even from father to son. Wan-sung notes, "In reality, this is no more even though a thousand Buddhas may emerge in the world, and no less even when a thousand sages pass away."
>
> When Lin-chi questioned his spiritual heir San-sheng, the latter showed his understanding that the Ch'an of Lin-chi is not a bunch of terms and doctrines and theories but direct experience of the indescribable reality that lies beyond our subjective imaginings. Wan-sung explains San-sheng's shout in this way: "When you don't stop what should be stopped, instead you bring about disorder." A mere follower might have mouthed off at Lin-chi's question, manifesting ignorance by trying to show understanding.

T'ien-t'ung said in verse:

The robe of faith imparted at midnight to a working man
Agitated the seven hundred monks of Yellow Plum;
The eye of truth of the Lin-chi branch
Perished with the blind ass, winning others' hatred.
Minds stamp each other, masters hand on the Lamp,
Leveling oceans and mountains,
Producing a giant bird.
This Itself cannot be named or said;
The whole method is knowing how to fly.

Yellow Plum is the name of the mountain associated with the community of the fifth patriarch of Ch'an Buddhism. Although he had seven hundred learned monastic disciples, the patriarch handed on the robe of the faith to an illiterate worker who had realized what is known as the knowledge that has no teacher. When they found out that a mere workman had gotten the patriarchate in preference to their learned selves, the seven hundred disciples were in an uproar. This classical story symbolizes the difference between acquired learning and direct perception, and how the former may actually impede the latter.

Minds stamp each other, masters hand on the Lamp: nothing is really given or received; Ch'an "transmission" is a mind-to-mind recognition. Only when the "student" has arrived at the stage of perception where this is possible can the "teacher" actually "recognize" their communication. Only the truly perceptive observer, furthermore, can distinguish this from suggestion and imitation.

The "shout" of San-sheng cut off all conceptual and doctrinal complications, "leveling oceans and mountains," at the same time manifesting the power of the realized man, "producing a giant bird." These are just metaphors, however, for what cannot be captured in conventional conceptualizations. The reality of direct perception of truth cannot actually be described, for it can only be known to the perceiver. There is no fixed way or path, for any means can become an end in the hands of the unenlightened; "the method is knowing how to fly," because direct perception is an experience of its own nature, only accessible to direct perception itself. You cannot "walk" on the legs of your ordinary conceptions from the ground of conventional reality to the sky of ultimate reality; it is necessary to be able to "fly" on the wings of ineffable awakening.

14. A Cup of Tea

Wan-sung says: "Probing pole in hand, surrounded by a reed blind, sometimes he wraps a ball of silk in iron, sometimes he wraps a special stone in silk. It is surely right to settle pliability by firmness; what about being weak when meeting strength?"

Testing is part of the process of Ch'an: seekers test teachers, teachers test seekers. One of the weaknesses of modern imitation Zen is the lack of accurate and adequate testing methods.

The probing pole and reed blind refer to indirect methods of testing through interaction. The combination and alternation of yielding and firmness characterizes the use of interaction to view people and situations from different angles.

Huo the attendant asked Te-shan, "Where have sages since time immemorial gone?"

Te-shan said, "Huh? What?"

Huo said, "The order was for a swift steed, but a lame slowpoke shows up."

Te-shan said nothing.

The next day, when Te-shan had come out of the bath, Huo handed him a cup of tea. Te-shan patted him on the back.

Huo said, "This old fellow has finally gotten a glimpse."

Again Te-shan said nothing.

The attendant was making his own fuss; this is what the teacher showed him. The teacher made no attempt at self-assertion; he would not rise to the attendant's bait to make some dogmatic pronouncement. One of the signs of a false teacher is the compulsion to play the role of the guru, with a ponderous crypticism for every occasion.

T'ien-t'ung said in verse:

Confronted face to face, one who's expert knows;
In this situation, even sparks and lightning are slow.
The strategist who lost his chance had an ulterior motive;
The militarist trying to fool the enemy didn't think ahead.
Each shot a sure hit,
Who would he take lightly?
If jowls are visible from behind, the man is not to be messed with;
He with his eyes beneath his brows is he who got the advantage.

> The first two lines depict Te-shan's adept handling of a double challenge. The third and fourth lines describe Huo's attempt to test Te-shan, instead being tested himself. The fifth and sixth lines point out that Te-shan's apparent casualness conceals a barb; he is not taking Huo's challenge lightly, even though he himself strikes home effortlessly. The last two lines conclude with the gist of Te-shan's practical lesson that Ch'an enlightenment is inconspicuous, true normalcy, not marked by exaggerations and oddities.

15. Planting a Hoe

Wan-sung says: "What is known before being spoken is called silent discourse; what becomes apparent of itself without clarification is called hidden potential. Greetings at the outside gate and pacing in the hallways have a measure of meaning; what about dancing in the yard or shaking the head outside the back door?"

> Mutual understanding outside the medium of verbal explanation is one of the specialties of Ch'an teaching. All sorts of fakery can and does enter into this silence, of course, so examination

and testing are also carried out. Greetings and pacing here stand for conventional activity; dancing and shaking the head represent unconventional activity. A member of a culture is able to discern accepted meanings within actions conventional to that culture; what about unconventional actions? Are nonconventional actions "meaningless," or do they have a special meaning?

Decadence and charlatanry in Zen are particularly rife in the area of the unconventional, as mindlessness degenerates into witlessness, and transcendence of the limitations of reason degenerates into irrationality. Therefore it is conventional to test the unconventional, even if it must be done by nonconventional as well as conventional means.

Kuei-shan asked Yang-shan, "Where are you coming from?"
Yang-shan replied, "From the fields."
Kuei-shan asked, "How many people are there in the fields?"
Yang-shan stuck his hoe in the ground, clasped his hands in salutation, and stood there.
Kuei-shan said, "There are a lot of people cutting reeds on South Mountain."
Yang-shan took up his hoe and went off.

Kuei-shan and Yang-shan were teacher and apprentice. In most stories featuring these two figures, the latter is already a master himself.

Where are you coming from? All of one's temporal being is taken in by this question, from cultural and personal history to psychological attitude to current activities.

In this story, Yang-shan is at the level of one who is no longer bound by personal or cultural history, and yet does not remain in the state of individual emancipation. At this point, he is "in the field," working in the world, and also returning to a source of higher knowledge, represented by the teacher Kuei-shan, for further refinement and expansion of his vision.

How many people are there in the fields? This is a question

122

about the general conditions in an area or domain of activity, and it also contains a question about the presence of people of insight at large. It can even be an invitation for the worker Yang-shan to show the "personalities" or "guest hosts" he employs to deal with the diversity of situations encountered in the world.

Planting his hoe in the ground, illustrating the secondary nature of temporal things and expedient devices, Yang-shan stands there with respect and dignity to reflect the solitary freedom of the independent individual.

Kuei-shan the teacher responds to this demonstration by pointing out that the full meaning of freedom, independence, and individuality lies in the contribution one makes, freely and independently, to the collective enterprise of Life, the business of being so, that is in any event going on at all times and in all places.

Like a good horse that need not be spurred, Yang-shan takes the hint. Picking up his hoe again, off he goes to work.

T'ien-t'ung said in verse:

The old illuminate's sentimental, thinking of his descendants;
Right now, he's embarrassed to have founded a house.
Let's remember the words about South Mountain,
Engraved on our bones, inscribed on our skin, as we render thanks
    together.

The first two lines caution the observer not to think of spiritual relationships in the same way as political, social, or emotional relationships. Confusion of the emotional with the spiritual is one of the distinguishing marks of imitation Zen cults today.

The last two lines remind the observer that the activity of Buddhist enlightenment, the rendering of gratitude to life for life, takes place in the context of life at large, in the company of all beings.

Shambhala Dragon Editions

The Art of War, by Sun Tzu. Translated by Thomas Cleary.
The Art of the Warrior: Leadership and Strategy from the Chinese Military Classics, translated by Ralph D. Sawyer.
The Awakened One: A Life of the Buddha, by Sherab Chödzin Kohn.
Bodhisattva of Compassion: The Mystical Tradition of Kuan Yin, by John Blofeld.
The Book of Five Rings, by Miyamoto Musashi. Translated by Thomas Cleary.
The Buddhist I Ching, by Chih-hsi Ou-i. Translated by Thomas Cleary.
Cutting Through Spiritual Materialism, by Chögyam Trungpa.
Dakini Teachings: Padmasambhava's Oral Instructions to Lady Tsogyal, by Padmasambhava. Translated by Erik Pema Kunsang.
The Diamond Sutra and The Sutra of Hui-neng. Translated by A. F. Price & Wong Mou-lam. Forewords by W. Y. Evans-Wentz & Christmas Humphreys.
The Essential Teachings of Zen Master Hakuin, translated by Norman Waddell.
The Experience of Insight: A Simple and Direct Guide to Buddhist Meditation, by Joseph Goldstein.
A Flash of Lightning in the Dark of Night: A Guide to the Bodhisattva's Way of Life, by Tenzin Gyatso, the Fourteenth Dalai Lama.
I Am Wind, You Are Fire: The Life and Work of Rumi, by Annemarie Schimmel.
Insight Meditation: The Practice of Freedom, by Joseph Goldstein.
Kensho: The Heart of Zen, by Thomas Cleary.
Lieh-tzu: A Taoist Guide to Practical Living, by Eva Wong.
Ling Ch'i Ching: A Classic Chinese Oracle, translated by Ralph D. Sawyer & Mei-chün Sawyer.
Living at the Source: Yoga Teachings of Vivekananda, by Swami Vivekananda.

(Continued on next page)

Living with Kundalini: The Autobiography of Gopi Krishna.

The Lotus-Born: The Life Story of Padmasambhava, by Yeshe Tsogyal. Translated by Erik Pema Kunsang.

Mastering the Art of War, by Zhuge Liang & Liu Ji. Translated & edited by Thomas Cleary.

The Mysticism of Sound and Music by Hazrat Inayat Khan.

The Myth of Freedom and the Way of Meditation, by Chögyam Trungpa.

Nine-Headed Dragon River, by Peter Matthiessen.

Rational Zen: The Mind of Dogen Zenji. Translated by Thomas Cleary.

Returning to Silence: Zen Practice in Daily Life, by Dainin Katagiri. Foreword by Robert Thurman.

Seeking the Heart of Wisdom: The Path of Insight Meditation, by Joseph Goldstein & Jack Kornfield. Foreword by H. H. the Dalai Lama.

Shambhala: The Sacred Path of the Warrior, by Chögyam Trungpa.

The Shambhala Dictionary of Buddhism and Zen.

The Spiritual Teaching of Ramana Maharshi, by Ramana Maharshi. Foreword by C. G. Jung.

Tao Teh Ching, by Lao Tzu. Translated by John C. H. Wu.

Teachings of the Buddha. Revised & expanded edition. Edited by Jack Kornfield.

The Tibetan Book of the Dead: The Great Liberation through Hearing in the Bardo. Translated with commentary by Francesca Fremantle & Chögyam Trungpa.

Vitality, Energy, Spirit: A Taoist Sourcebook. Translated & edited by Thomas Cleary.

The Way of the Bodhisattva: A Translation of the Bodhicharyavatara, by Shantideva. Translated by the Padmakara Translation Group.

Wen-tzu: Understanding the Mysteries, by Lao-tzu. Translated by Thomas Cleary.

Zen Essence: The Science of Freedom. Translated & edited by Thomas Cleary.

Zen Teachings of Master Lin-chi. Translated by Burton Watson.